/ 4

The emotions that World War I evoke are often contradictory. It can be seen as a time when men and women believed in the causes they were fighting for, yet on the other hand it can be viewed as a war in which many elite generals used their forces stupidly. Some have said the fighting in that time before nuclear weapons was cleaner than that which we are threatened with now. Others say that the trench warfare conducted during the conflict was the ugliest, most bloody fighting civilized man has ever known. No matter which position seems valid, anyone interested in why we live the way we do today must be interested in World War I. And what better way to learn about history than to study the men and women who lived it? Here, then, are portraits of twelve men and women both little-known and famous who contributed to this crucial time in the history of the modern world.

ERICH LUDENDORFF: He led the German troops on their brutal march through Belgium and France.

GENERAL JOFFRE: The old general who rose to the defense of France.

(Continued on back flap)

BOLD LEADERS
OF
WORLD WAR I

BY
COLONEL RED REEDER

LITTLE, BROWN AND COMPANY
BOSTON   TORONTO

FIRST EDITION

T10/74

Library of Congress Cataloging in Publication Data
Reeder, Russell Potter.
  Bold leaders of World War I.
  CONTENTS: The two world wars: the differences.—Erich Luden-
dorff, general at the gates.—[etc.]—Bibliography (p.   )
  1. European   War,   1914–1918—Biography—Juvenile   literature.
[1. European War, 1914–1918—Biography] I. Title.
D507.R37   940.3'092'2   [B]   [920]   74-13492
ISBN 0-316-73671-6

Published simultaneously in Canada
by Little, Brown & Company (Canada) Limited

PRINTED IN THE UNITED STATES OF AMERICA

For
my son
Russell Potter Reeder III

Acknowledgments

When I write a book, I need help. I was fortunate in writing this one to receive outstanding assistance from my wife, Dort Darrah Reeder. She not only typed these stories several times and corrected my grammar, but she counseled me and prepared the index, as she did for my other books. Mr. Egon Weiss, Mr. Alan Aimone, Colonel John R. Elting, Mr. and Mrs. Gene Leone, Dr. Forrest C. Pogue, Bishop Fulton J. Sheen, and Rear Admiral Fred M. Reeder also assisted.

Brigadier General R. P. ("Doc") Eaton gave me a vivid picture of his part in the war. Members of the late William Breckenridge's family of eastern Canada, James and George, furnished information enabling me to develop parts of William's unusual manuscript, "From Vimy to Mons." I am grateful to James Breckenridge for permission to use that work.

I thank Mr. David C. ("Spec") McClure for access to his unpublished and valuable manuscript about Laurence Stallings: "The Man Who Refused to Die."

I also received information for the Stallings story from Colonel Frank C. Caldwell, deputy director of Marine Corps history.

In Lexington, Virginia, Dr. Forrest C. Pogue, Mr. Royster Lyle, and Miss Diane Elliot, all of the George C. Marshall Research Foundation, made original sources and files available on George C. Marshall.

Colonel John H. F. Haskell sent me information from Brussels on Edith Cavell. Miss Charlotte Snyder, on the staff of the United States Military Academy Library, assisted, too, in obtaining information about Edith Cavell and on other subjects in this book.

I thank the *Morning Post*, the *Daily Telegraph*, both of London, and Mr. Frederick Woods for permission to include a passage from Mr. Woods' *Young Winston's Wars*.

I am also grateful to Mrs. T. S. Riggs, Jr., Mrs. Dale Hruby, Colonel Elbert E. Farman, Jr., Lieutenant General William A. Knowlton, Major General William M. Creasy, and Brigadier General B. P. Heiser for information. I thank others also, whom I cannot list, for helping me along the way.

In his usual expert fashion, Mr. Edward J. Krasnoberski drew the map showing Mannerheim's amazing ride.

Red Reeder

Contents

Introduction

For one to truly understand the intensity of the war fever of 1914–1918, one had to live in those years. At its start, World War I was a crusade. Enthusiasm for fighting marked the entrance of each nation as it took the plunge into war.

The zeal stirring the United States seemed akin to the feeling that had roused American patriots from their beds along the route of the Redcoats when they marched out of Boston in 1775 for Lexington and Concord.

In 1917 and early 1918, with many thousands of Americans being shipped to training camps and to France, the same eagerness for battle spread from state to state. Bands in theaters and in parades specialized in playing "Over There," and flags flew everywhere, every day; ministers thundered from pulpits on the evilness of the enemy; and you felt like a traitor if you were doing nothing to help your country.

When I was sixteen, the excitement of war fever and

a sense of duty gripped me. I said, "Mother, I want to enlist."

"No," she said. "Your father and your uncle in France are enough for our family. I need you at home to help take care of your two sisters, your brother, and me." She and the younger children suddenly took on a fresh importance because of my new responsibilities. I have been forever grateful for her decision.

Excitement multiplied in the United States. I was in Baltimore when a detachment of Alpine chasseurs from France paraded through the streets at a quick-step. Horizon-blue overcoats, capes pinned back at the shoulders exposing cerulean-blue linings. Sleeves ornamented with gold wound chevrons. Red kepis. The tricolor. Officers' swords sparkling in the sun. Curved horns blowing stirring calls to the rumble of drums. Crowds on the sidewalks applauding and cheering. I ran alongside in a crowd of boys, watching the heroes eat up ground. The soldiers were advertising a loan for France. It was unthinkable not to give money.

The feeling became so intense in America that even dachshunds were stoned. My brother Fred's nickname was Fritz. When he was eight in 1915, he announced, "Everybody listen! From now on my name is Fred." A nursemaid herding us around, who happened to be a German *fräulein*, once forgot and called him Fritz. He lay down on a New York City sidewalk on Park Avenue in protest. I was very proud of him.

This book is about some of the unique people — all of them leaders, whether great or small — who, not unlike my brother, felt deeply about the war: two Britons, a Canadian, two Frenchmen, two Germans, an Austrian, a Finn who fought for the Russians and then against them, and three Americans.

BOLD LEADERS

OF

WORLD WAR I

1

THE TWO WORLD WARS
The Differences

PERHAPS, years from now, the two world wars will be considered as one war. Indeed, the German historian Fritz Fischer has suggested that World War I was merely the introductory phase of the "greater Germany" of Hitler and his Nazi party.

The two wars followed close upon each other. World War I began in 1914 and ended in 1918. World War II started only twenty-one years later, in 1939, and lasted until 1945.

One's mind cannot grasp the enormous fatalities incurred in the two world wars. Historians list the number of men killed in action, missing, or dead of wounds as 9,981,000 in World War I (this figure does not include Turkish losses, which are unknown) and 16,698,775 in World War II.

The introduction speaks of the enthusiasm at the start of the first of the two conflicts. Before 1914 the brutally frank speeches of Kaiser Wilhelm II had disclosed that Germany was soon going to take the war-

path. Consequently, it was no problem for govern-
ments and individuals to see what was coming and to
foment excitement — although not all people favored
war. For instance, the Scotch-Canadians who lived
along the shore of Lake Erie opposed it, as did many
Americans of German descent. And a handful of prominent United States citizens — Jane Addams, William
Jennings Bryan, Henry Ford, Senator Robert Marion
La Follette — vehemently declared many times that
they wanted no bloodshed by their countrymen, regardless of what disaster occurred in Europe.

Although thinking people could see World War I
approaching, World War II arrived almost by stealth;
many people refused to see the peril of Hitler and his
Nazis. Europeans remembered the casualties of World
War I, and when World War II started, they had no
illusions about what they were getting into. Enthusiasm at the start of the first conflict and lack of it in the
second marked an important difference between the
wars.

In World War I, the miserable trenches extending
from the sea to Switzerland, marring Western Europe,
were distinguishing marks of the conflict. Out of these
ditches sprang disastrous massive attacks across shell-
pocked No-Man's-Land, where "progress" was usually
marked in yards. One of the worst examples of the
slaughter of trench warfare occurred at Passchendaele,
Belgium, in 1917, when the British general Sir Douglas Haig, not realizing that during his career times had
changed and that machine guns were ruling the battle-

field, ordered his soldiers to attack straight ahead in order to capture German trenches protected by lines of machine guns. Winston Churchill said, "Britain bled herself white at Passchendaele." The loss of many thousands of virile young men during World War I contributed to the beginning of the end of the British Empire. In the major countries of the world, life has never been the same since then.

In World War I, poison gases took their toll. The trenches, particularly in the West, were bordered with hundreds of miles of barbed wire. On the Eastern Front, heavy fighting and organized sabotage toppled the Russian monarchy, and the Russian people were finally gripped by Communism. The war cost Russia and Germany approximately three million men each.

There were epic struggles in World War I. For instance, in the fields and forts around Verdun, France, almost one million Germans and Frenchmen were killed, wounded, or captured. And airmen entered combat for the first time. There was fighting on the sea and under it, in the Arctic, in the Balkans and Turkey, and in the deserts of Mesopotamia.

In World War I, the United States entered the war on the side of the Allies — the British, French, Italians, and Russians — declaring war against Germany on April 6, 1917, only after German submarines had fired their deadly fish into United States ships. Many of these were supply vessels carrying war materials to Allied ports. U.S. orators and writers vowed that "freedom of the seas is being violated." Propaganda on both sides played a part; Americans were assured that they were entering "a war to end all wars."

No one can say how many civilians were lost in each war. Whole populations were displaced and destroyed in World War II. Over five million Jews were put to death by Hitler and his bloodthirsty Nazis. Cities were ruined by aerial bombing. Battles raged over the entire European continent. Only Switzerland, Sweden, and Spain were spared. Many square miles of Russia, Africa, the Far East, the Arctic, the Mediterranean, the Atlantic and Pacific oceans, and prominent islands, including England, came under attack from 1939 to 1945.

Hitler's ambition sparked World War II. The United States finally plunged actively into the war on December 7, 1941, when Japanese planes surprised and sank a large part of the United States fleet at Pearl Harbor, Hawaii. World War II ended with the destruction of two Japanese cities by atomic bombs.

But although the losses of World War II were greater, for soldiers World War I was the worst combat of modern times.

After its close in 1918, Prime Minister Lloyd George summed up the trial of Britain's fighting men, and indeed his remarks apply to the warriors in each army:

"There never has been in the history of mankind such a courage as our soldiers displayed. It was not valour they displayed, it was not even heroism; it was something so new and terrible, so undreamed of, that man has created no new word for it. The nearest word

I can get is Endurance. They were in hell every day of their lives. They were exposed to all the nerve-shattering rage of artillery, artillery which rived the soil like an earthquake, which hurled the bodies of the dead into the air, and flung the bodies of the living into a deeper sepulchre; and they endured.

"Yes, they endured, endured inexpressible agony with patience, even with humor, and at the end they beat the enemy to his knees. There has been nothing like this in the history of the world."

The stories that follow show the toil, the agony, the patience, and in some cases the humor, that Lloyd George spoke of.

2

ERICH LUDENDORFF
General at the Gates

ALTHOUGH THE WAR had just begun, the German war plan was crumbling. General Erich Ludendorff, a leader with tremendous will power but one crammed to the gills with conceit, listened to the dismal reports pouring into supreme headquarters. "If I can just get to the advance guard," he told staff officers, "I can repair the trouble."

The officers had mixed feelings. They were well acquainted with Ludendorff's unusual ability but also with his overwhelming egotism.

In the first days of the war, the German spearhead had barged into Belgium and had met with only a little resistance, which had been easily brushed aside. Now, at Liège, forty thousand Belgians in forts had stopped sixty thousand especially selected Germans in their tracks. This was the "trouble" Ludendorff was talking about.

The Germans had started their invasion of Belgium

confidently — and they had marched into southern
Holland and Luxembourg at the same time — with
flags flying, bands playing, and the soldiers singing
such songs as "Die Wacht am Rhein." But presently
they were suffering numerous casualties and their
leaders were confused. Determined Belgian resistance
was not in the "enemy reaction" part of the German
plan.

Ludendorff was a vigorous, ambitious officer. Long
years of hard work and training had moved him from
one high position to another in the Kaiser's army, and
now he agonized because Belgians in and around Liège
had upset the German invasion timetable. He also suffered from a gnawing personal disappointment: he was
not in command of anything.

Ludendorff began his drive for the top at the age of
twelve, when he entered the Ploener Military Academy in northern Germany near the Baltic Sea. He had
been raised in the beautiful East Prussia country, and
it seemed only natural that he should attend Ploener —
he wanted a military career. His father was a common
businessman, neither wealthy nor powerful, and young
Ludendorff secretly despised his father's simple background. At Ploener, Erich's fellow cadets lost no time
in teasing him because his name lacked the "von" of
nobility. Their ridicule caused him to withdraw from
the group and increased his desire to succeed.

He was also influenced by the unyielding Prussian
officers who governed the cadets. The officers preferred
facing a bear rather than an excuse. They set examples

General Erich von Ludendorff. (United Press Inter-national Photo)

in devotion to duty, but also in arrogance. Extreme haughtiness toward subordinates and civilians was a characteristic. The Prussians had the humility of tigers in a jungle.

In a feudal atmosphere, the officers demanded top performance from the cadets in everything from shining boots and bayonets to grades in academic subjects. At night, it was put your elbows on the table and study until a drummer signaled "Lamps out." The cadets gave instant and unquestioning obedience like vassals to their lord.

The cadets concentrated on military drawing (a study relieved by reconnoitering on horseback), bird's-eye-view sketches, the organization of the army, regulations, the history of tactics, fortifications, the manufacture of weapons, the care of gunpowder, and so on. The boys received few lectures. In class, they stood rigidly at attention and recited. There was no competition between cadets, but a boy who did not do his best in his academic work received no privileges and was punished. Games of chance that might cause injury were forbidden. Dueling, common in German civilian schools, was outlawed. A board of honor settled quarrels and punished aggressors. Nineteenth-century German military academies raised a serious-minded set of cadets.

Ludendorff, who desperately wanted a military career, proved outstanding in everything except gymnastics. He felt mortified because he could not chin himself and because his efforts on the long horse made the cadets howl. He handled himself with all the grace of a beer barrel.

Ludendorff proved intelligent; he was a top student both at Ploener and at the higher Lichterfelde Military Academy in Berlin. At eighteen, in 1882, he received a commission as a lieutenant in the Marines. His ruthless drive, unquenchable ambition, and devotion to duty skyrocketed him to the top of the list of officers on the general staff. He became well known throughout the German army as an uncompromising soldier to whom hours meant nothing and who could solve difficult problems. True, he had few friends. There had been no time for that: the work and study required of officers on the general staff were too demanding.

These officers reported only to the commanding general of the army. Carefully selected, carefully trained, tested and retested, they concentrated on enemy intelligence (such as the secret plans to defend Liège), on military strategy, and on how to supply armies. They took pride in the special, wine-red stripe down their trousers that marked them as a corps apart. They were devoted to Germany, the Kaiser, the senior general of the army, and to their own prestige.

Erich Ludendorff developed into a humorless leader with a one-track mind. He believed in the creed that all one had to do to succeed was to work and carry out orders.

Although he was devoted to his wife and family, and depended upon them for moral support, in his climb to the top of the general staff he turned his home into a place reserved for eating, sleeping and work. His wife often told the children that their father had come home looking like a glacier. She and the children were well disciplined. Each evening, no talking was the rule while Ludendorff studied papers from a briefcase that an enlisted man had delivered after supper. (It was beneath the dignity of a German officer to carry luggage or parcels.) Ludendorff's medical director summed him up: "He has never seen a flower bloom or heard a bird sing."

As a member of the general staff, Ludendorff had been presented to Kaiser Wilhelm II. Like his military colleagues, Ludendorff approved of the Kaiser's flagrant preference for military leaders over chiefs of industry and civil authorities. The Kaiser, after all, headed the German state, and the generals saw nothing amiss when he appeared in uniform at public functions and when he said, "These are *my* soldiers and sailors and *my* officers. . . . Everything I do is right. I am carrying out the Will of God." And, as 1914 approached, the Kaiser said, "War is inevitable." The Kaiser, god of the German army, predicted that the war would be over and his troops home "before the leaves fall from the trees."

The fact that peaceful Belgium, Holland, and Luxembourg lay in the path of the German invasion did not bother the Kaiser or his military leaders. Chancellor Theobald von Bethmann-Hollweg, head of the Kaiser's civilian government, who had tried to stop the slide toward war, proved as ineffective as a candle in a gale.

The Kaiser and his senior generals had adopted a secret plan, which had been brewed back in 1905 by the famous military writer Count Alfred von Schlieffen. His idea was that a fast offensive, crashing through Belgium into the "backdoor of France," would be the first step in gaining victory and in ending the war rapidly. Obviously, if it dragged on, German military prestige would suffer. Before the count died, he warned German generals time and again, "Make certain we crush France with a *lightning attack* before the Russian steamroller gets started. Make the right wing strong." After defeating France, Germany would turn and wipe out the Russian armies. But first the German attack had to capture the stronghold at Liège.

In preparing for war, the great German general staff and its superiors had duped themselves by swallowing reports from well-meaning and well-paid spies that Liège was weak. Capturing the city and its forts was vital to the success of the invasion because supplies for three attacking German armies had to pass through the twelve-mile gap that the guns of Liège controlled.

The spies had not understood the spirit of the Belgian king Albert, a man loved by his people. Nor had the Kaiser, in his arrogance, counted on Albert's dauntlessness, a courage strengthened before the invasion when the Kaiser sent him a carrot-and-stick note: "Any damages by the Kaiser's soldiers will be paid for, and if the Belgians show good will the independence of their kingdom is guaranteed. However, any act of resistance will be regarded as an act of the enemy."

This deadly message made King Albert determined to pit his little army against the Kaiser's hordes; after all, the defense had advantages. This was why the Belgian fortress at Liège, in the hot August of 1914, was stopping the advance guard of the German army.

On the fifth of August, General Ludendorff and an aide traveled in an open touring car through army traffic toward the Front. Tired German soldiers slumping on the side of the road indicated to Ludendorff that something was wrong. When he stopped to inquire, he could find only junior officers, who knew nothing. Their excuse, "Something wrong up front near Liège, Herr General," was extremely unsatisfactory.

As the important first quartermaster general, Ludendorff was responsible for food, other supplies, transportation, and clothing. But with his restless drive he was going up to the front to see for himself what the immediate difficulties were, something he felt other senior generals should have been doing. He hungered for command.

Ludendorff drove to a hilltop on the outskirts of Liège, where the battlefield was spread out below him. Shells from German artillery were baptizing with iron the forts, the pillboxes, and trenches guarding the city. Belgian artillery was almost being overpowered, but it was firing at the invaders. The noise sounded like a violent thunderstorm.

Ludendorff's field glasses let him peer through the haze and smoke rising from Liège factories and from the battle. On the far side of the Meuse River, German cavalry, fighting on foot, were assaulting the Belgian forts. To the north, peasants were running from blazing farm buildings near the stream.

Just as General Otto von Emmich joined him on the hill, a white flag appeared on the ramparts of the citadel, the principal fort some two miles away. Emmich rejoiced. "Wonderful! Now our armies can proceed. I'll send an officer at once under a flag of truce to see about the surrender."

Ludendorff disapproved, but as he had no authority to command he could only suggest: "Why not wait until they send an envoy to us?"

But Emmich insisted, and soon his aide rode into the town — only to return crestfallen. He saluted Emmich and reported, "Herr General, the white flag on the citadel was a mistake."

A brigade of gray-clad German infantry, wearing spiked helmets and packs, tried to advance in short rushes toward the forts. Their rifles sounded like a giant ripping cardboard, but the sound was feeble compared to the increased fire that the Belgians poured out of the pillboxes. The German brigade seemed helpless. Part of the trouble was that it had taken a thousand prisoners, who hindered its movements and were like stones around its neck.

The German zeppelin "LZ," an airship as long as two and a half football fields, purred over Liège and tried vainly to bomb the city into surrendering. The six engines of the zeppelin and the explosions of the bombs sounded like a weird hymn of death.

The sinking sun colored the town and the citadel dull red, except for scarlet tongues of flame from fires started by the zeppelin. Some German units deployed on the plain below the hill were in disorder as Belgian guns pounded them with bullets and iron shell fragments. Count von Schlieffen had foreseen nothing like this. Confusion began to infect the German ranks.

With darkness shrouding the battlefield, the bright streaks of yellow searchlights cut through the night. The terrible spectacle was like a bad dream for Ludendorff. He stumbled down the hill to the nearest German infantry company. When the headlights of a staff car picked him out the soldiers cheered. They felt buoyed up at seeing a general so close to the fighting. They swarmed about the car as he climbed in, yelling, "We'll be in Liège tomorrow." Their enthusiasm, in turn, braced the general.

Ludendorff did not feel as confident after entering a farmhouse, three miles back, which was serving as a division headquarters. The gloom there was so thick you could cut it with a knife. Shadows on the walls from an oil lamp looked grotesque. The only man in the room with a smile was a corporal who handed out bowls of soup from the farmer's kitchen.

A major with a sorrowful face showed Ludendorff a fistful of papers and said, "Nobody's moving forward,

Herr General. The most important report is on the door."

Nailed to the door by a spike was a radio message, printed on pink paper:

From: KING ALBERT
To: GENERAL GERARD LEMAN, COMMANDING THE
        LIÈGE DEFENSES. I CHARGE YOU TO HOLD TO THE
        END THE POSITION YOU HAVE BEEN ENTRUSTED TO
        DEFEND.

                                              ALBERT

The farmhouse shook as four German howitzers, in a nearby field, thundered shells into the city. Dirt from the rafters rained on the officers and ruined Ludendorff's soup. He barked above the noise at the headquarters commandant, "What you need is instruction in how to select a headquarters building."

Bad news poured in. Casualty reports were higher than the general staff had predicted. Then word arrived that a night attack had fizzled. Shortly, the lieutenant colonel of a nearby battalion stamped in, blaming the failure on Belgian *francs-tireurs* (civilian snipers) who fired into his battalion in the morning and who had managed to slay most of his officers. These outrageous civilians were being rounded up and would be shot without trial, the colonel said.

Ludendorff gave his opinion of the *francs-tireurs*: "They're enough to disgust any soldier. I, myself, this afternoon, saw uniforms they discarded. They've broken the rules of war."

There was also distress on the road by the farm-house. German soldiers were trudging by, carrying wounded to the rear, instead of leaving that responsi-bility to the hospital corpsmen. This violated orders. They had to be made to realize that the way to victory lay through Liège.

A cyclist entered the building, saluted an adjutant, and handed him a priority message. The officers read by lamplight: "A shell from Liège has killed General Wussow, commanding the Fourteenth Brigade."

Ludendorff decided to act.

Early the next morning he plodded across country hoping to reach Colonel von Oven, in charge of the German advance guard. If he could find the colonel, he could start the attack on a better course. Soldiers told Ludendorff that the colonel had gone to capture the fortress.

Ludendorff commandeered a captured Belgian car, climbed in it with an adjutant, drove across one of the few bridges left standing, and sped toward the citadel. Suddenly, the chauffeur jammed on the brakes. The iron gates of the citadel, twenty yards away, were bolted. On a small flagpole nearby fluttered the verti-cal black, yellow, and red stripes of the Belgian flag.

Ludendorff jumped out. He drew his sword as if he were attacking the fort single-handed. He pounded on the gate with the hilt of his weapon and shouted, "Sur-render! In the name of Kaiser Wilhelm."

Amazingly, the gates creaked open. Ludendorff strutted in as if he were on parade. The Belgian guards

crashed their rifles to a salute as the citadel surrendered to him.

It is hard to know Ludendorff's feelings. He concealed them that day and, in his writings later,
summed up his amazing capture in twenty-five words:
"I banged on the gates, which were locked. They were
opened from the inside. The few hundred Belgians
who were there surrendered at my summons." In his
book *War Memories*, he did say, "This capture is the
favorite recollection of my life."

Although white sheets soon draped the citadel's ramparts as a signal to other forts that it had surrendered,
other Belgian positions held. The Germans knew how
to bring them down. Teams of horses tugged up gigantic Austrian Skoda siege guns, twelve inches in diameter in the muzzle, as well as scores of 150 mm howitzers. The heavy artillery poured shells into the
defenses.

By August 16, 1914, Liège and its supporting bul-
warks had either crumpled or surrendered. The
Kaiser's spearhead reorganized and swept on, with the
armies following.

Later there were claims and counterclaims as to how
much the Belgians had upset the German timetable
and had gained valuable time for the confused French.
The defenders of Liège threw the juggernaut off sched-
ule anywhere from two to five days. And when many of
the Belgians fell back on Antwerp, they caused General Alexander von Kluck, the German commander, to
send thousands of men from his right wing to contain
them.

The Germans marked their invasion of Belgium with atrocities. Infuriated by *francs-tireurs*, the invaders hauled priests and other innocents before firing squads. Columns of black smoke, from burning homes and farms, signaled the German advance. In Louvain, fifty miles from Liège, almost every house felt the torch, and for good measure drunken soldiers fired into the buildings. Louvain's world-famous library, containing seven hundred and fifty medieval manuscripts and almost a quarter-million books, went up in flames. St. Peter's Church looked as if it had been sacked by the Vandals of the first century. Food became a dreadful problem in the raped city. General Helmuth von Moltke, charged by the Kaiser with implementing the Schlieffen plan, understatedly wrote, "Our advance through Belgium is certainly brutal." Allied propaganda writers reached for their pens, exaggerating the wantonness of the invaders, although in truth no need for overstatement existed.

Berliners went crazy with joy over both the march through Belgium and into France, and General Ludendorff's bold performance. His country hailed him. His daring act seemed symbolic of what it could expect from its military leaders. The Kaiser himself pinned the rare *Ordre pour le Mérite* on Ludendorff's chest and offered him promotion to second chief of the general staff.

Ludendorff declined with thanks. He did not want to be second to anything. He would rather remain *first* quartermaster general.

Erich Ludendorff, hero of the capture of Liège, was

eventually carried higher in the German army by his ambition and drive, and he served his country on increasing planes of importance. He became part of the powerful Hindenberg-Ludendorff team on the Russian Front — two leaders who worked so closely and effectively that they were at times characterized by the logotype **HL** .

Eventually Ludendorff reached supreme command of German forces on the Western Front, but his narrowness led him into mistakes that hastened Germany's loss of the war and cost her many thousands of lives.

By August 1918, this man of iron will finally realized that Germany had lost the war. He called for an armistice. His disappointment made him half crazy, and he was forced to resign.

In 1923, hoping to vault once more into power, Ludendorff cast his lot with Hitler and the Nazis. This led him into various unsuccessful civic risings. Although Ludendorff was a superb organizer, he could not succeed in the political arena. He died, a bitter man, in Munich in 1937.

3

PAPA JOFFRE
and the German Claw

WHEN FIVE GERMAN ARMIES swept down from the north in the form of a huge claw, in August 1914, France was depending upon the leadership of General Joffre.

Not every Frenchman felt sure of the sixty-two-year-old general, who appeared to be anything but a dashing leader. A baggy uniform failed to conceal his medicine-ball stomach, and his unkempt white walrus mustache, hiding a smile that he sometimes permitted himself, added to the illusion that he might be a clod.

In 1914, officers in every army improved the smartness of their appearance by wearing trim boots. Joffre's boots possessed the grace of two stovepipes. The only perky part of his uniform was his gaudy kepi, ringed by three bands of gold laurel leaves, but he jammed this blood-red cap down on his bushy white hair as if he expected a whirlwind. The visor and Joffre's bushy eyebrows shielded calm blue eyes. A square chin and a

King Victor Emmanuel of Italy (left) and General Joseph Joffre at the Italian front. (United Press International Photo)

broad nose with flared nostrils hinted at obstinacy. He had obstinacy to spare.

Joseph Jacques Césaire Joffre looked like a retired traffic policeman, but he acted like a czar. His soldiers grinned when they talked of him, calling him "Grand-père" and "Papa." His generals walked warily, knowing that if they failed to turn in a top performance they would be out of a job. The army believed him to be smart. Insiders also realized that the old general fought to control a flash-like temper.

It was not Joffre's temper that had irritated Georges Clemenceau, known as the Tiger, but the general's obstinacy and aloofness, bordering on rudeness.

Clemenceau, the former Premier of France, lived for the day when France would gain revenge against the Germans for the defeat in the War of 1870. He had approached Papa Joffre with ideas on how to better the French army, but the general had listened and merely shrugged. Joffre was sure that he knew more about military life than any politician, and he decided that if he talked to Clemenceau he would just be outargued.

When Joffre did condescend to answer the Tiger, he spoke in a low voice tinged by a Spanish accent acquired as a boy in the foothills of the Pyrenees. Joffre's opinionated mind shunted Clemenceau aside, making an enemy of the odd-looking man with the high cheekbones and sallow skin. The Tiger decided that there would come a time when he would cut Joffre down.

Members of the press thought Papa Joffre an enigma and some said that he belonged in an earlier age. When reporters questioned officers about him, they pointed out that he was above politics — unique in a country where politics was almost a sport. One volunteered, "General Joffre is a Freemason. But if need be, he'd punish a Freemason as quickly as he would a Catholic."

Joffre had been schooled by the Jesuits, priests dedicated to their order. Their devotion was reflected in Joffre's character. No one was more dedicated to France than Papa Joffre. But Joffre's military record contained a serious flaw. Although he had proved his bravery on the battlefield as a second lieutenant in 1870, and although his work as an engineering officer had been superb, and although he was known to be trustworthy, he lacked staff training. Consequently, his ideas about how a large headquarters should work were vague. Joffre was aware of his deficiency and perhaps worried about it; it handicapped him in dealing with his fifty assistants. Often the harassed officers did not know what he wanted. But they could be sure of one thing: Papa Joffre was very slow to change his mind.

Joffre was the senior officer of the French army at a time when it cherished a dangerous doctrine: *"Toujours l'attaque"* — always attack. This seemed to be the answer to the hardest problem of war: leading men to victory on the battlefield. After all, *Napoleon had formed his empire by attacking.* The trouble was that the formula did not consider that at certain times it might be smart to adopt the defensive, and it did not allow for changing battlefield conditions.

Joffre's trouble began before the war started, when he drew up a plan, based on *l'attaque*, with which to defeat the Germans if they invaded France. He would cut up the enemy and win back the "lost provinces" of Alsace and Lorraine, territory torn from France in the War of 1870. Joffre had decided that if war came he would send two armies to defeat the Germans in the east, recapturing the lost provinces, and a small army to block any enemies who might filter through Belgium. Joffre felt confident of his idea. He called it Plan 17. It was as faulty as a foundation made with poor concrete.

Most of Joffre's other thoughts, however, were far from faulty. For instance, he believed that soldiers who possessed high morale, discipline, and esprit de corps were almost sure to win. This idea had been advanced by Colonel Ardant du Picq, a military thinker and a brave soldier of 1870. Du Picq had harped on esprit de corps, and in 1914 the uniform of the French soldiers seemed related to it.

The soldiers wore blue coats, red kepis (like Joffre's except for the rings of gold laurel leaves), and scarlet trousers. Once in civilian debate, when it had been suggested that such a gaudy combination offered a target for the enemy and consequently the uniform should be changed, Eugène Etienne, the French Minister of War, jumped to his feet and shouted, *"Jamais! Le pantalon rouge c'est la France!"* (Never! The red trousers are France!)

In 1914 the morale, discipline, and esprit de corps of

the French soldiers was at the top. Their training had
given them confidence. They felt sure that as long as
Papa Joffre called the tune they could make the Germans dance.

On August 14, with war under way, Papa Joffre sent
long columns of French soldiers toiling over the roads
to Alsace-Lorraine. From a distance, the formations
looked like huge, strange caterpillars with red legs.
Right behind the infantry, horses tugged the famous
French 75's (cannon with bores a little less than three
inches wide), the finest field-artillery piece in the
world. Recapturing Alsace-Lorraine seemed assured.

But to the north of Paris the situation was growing
more perilous by the hour. Hordes of Germans poured
through Belgium, marching south toward the heart of
France. General Charles Lanrezac, the French commander near the Belgian border, hurried away from
the fighting to confer with General Joffre. Lanrezac
worried. He knew that Papa Joffre was stubborn.
Could he make him see the danger?

In the meantime, Joffre's staff was having trouble —
with Joffre. It was not easy to get to him. No one felt
brave enough to disturb him if an important message
arrived while he was eating. When Joffre was a boy,
one of a family of eleven, food had been scarce, and
now under fearful pressure he was shoveling in nour-
ishment. His favorite between-meal snack was goose
liver, and his chefs had to stock it. Sometimes he took
naps after meals. The war could wait. One wag libeled
him later by saying, "This is where General Joffre

slept before the Battle of the Marne, after the battle, and during the battle."

When General Lanrezac stepped out of his car at Joffre's headquarters, he resembled a frustrated professor. Lanrezac lost no time; he challenged the sacred Plan 17.

Papa Joffre tugged on his white mustache. "How many Germans are coming through Belgium?"

Lanrezac adjusted his steel-rimmed eyeglasses nervously. "It is hard, *mon général*, to determine exactly how many Germans. They have their own cavalry screen out in front. I'm sure, very positive, that I am up against their main effort."

The tall, gaunt Lanrezac paced about Joffre's office, waving his hands at the map, talking faster and faster, begging to be allowed to move his army into Belgium. "I need more help, more help."

"We need more help everywhere," Joffre shrugged.

Lanrezac raved on. Finally Papa Joffre interrupted and ended the meeting by grunting, "You worry too much. It is my responsibility to stop the Germans."

In spite of Lanrezac's plea, Joffre pushed his Plan 17 as hard as he could, moving into Alsace-Lorraine, where the Germans were withdrawing in order to entice him into a trap. He would not bring himself to believe that there were German armies smashing down from the north with the idea of cutting behind him as he pushed into Alsace-Lorraine.

The Germans were not only fighting but were spreading propaganda leaflets that had been drawn up in the neutral states of Holland and Switzerland. One read:

> *Frenchmen! What do you know about Alsace-Lorraine? Most of the territory Germany is supposed to have "robbed" from France in 1870 was actually robbed from Germany by an invasion of that French tyrant, Louis XIV. The provinces and population are German. If the French are so sure that Alsace-Lorrainers wish to become French, why do they object to a popular vote?*

In 1914, German propaganda had little effect on French soldiers. The leaflets hinted at political schemes and few Frenchmen were interested in political affairs at such a grave hour.

However, when General Lanrezac arrived back with his army near Belgium, he felt as if he were plunged into international politics. The British Expeditionary Force, one hundred thousand strong, had crossed the English Channel to attack the Germans. It took General Lanrezac but a few hours to discover that the leader of the BEF, Sir John French, a dedicated but testy British bulldog as old as Joffre, had a serious failing: he could not get along with people.

Sir John, a fine soldier at one time, wore his sensitivity on his sleeve. And it had been impressed upon him that he was to cooperate with the French but that he was to fight independently of their orders — dangerous instructions to give an old general with an ingrown, stunted personality.

When Sir John and General Lanrezac talked, the French general, dead tired and under the powerful pressure of the enemy, gave off sparks like flint struck by steel. The English general reacted, sticking out his chin almost as if Charles Lanrezac represented the Germans. The two leaders soon despised each other.

In the meantime, the hundred thousand British soldiers under Sir John — "the contemptible little army," the Kaiser called it — were moving north by boxcars and by marching, searching for the enemy. When the British columns, wearing drab, mud-colored uniforms and singing "Tipperary," swung through French villages, the townspeople greeted them with food and flowers as if they were saviors. "No wine," Sir John ordered, and his men obeyed. This was a disciplined, dedicated army, determined to stop the "Huns," as they called the Germans.

When the British "Tommies," hiking north, met swarms of French and Belgian refugees, hurrying to escape hard-riding German uhlans, the singing stopped. There was chaos on the roads. An uprooted French population of grandfathers, grandmothers, mothers, and children plodded south alongside farm wagons and every type of vehicle they could command — even dog-carts. Babies rode in hand-pushed carriages or in the luggage. The BEF wanted the road. So did the refugees.

The situation was just as grave at headquarters. The two allied leaders, Sir John and General Lanrezac, were expected to cooperate, but they were equal in rank and each possessed an abundance of pride. Their clash began to hinder the Allied effort.

When the confused situation became so grave that the two leaders had to confer again, they met privately. No interpreters were present because of the fetish for secrecy, yet neither general could speak the other's language! Sir John owned a summer home in Normandy, but he could sputter only a few phrases in French. The overbearing, excitable Lanrezac couldn't speak a word of English.

When their conference fizzled, they called for interpreters, but even then misunderstandings arose. Sir John asked Lanrezac where he thought the Germans would cross the Meuse River. Lanrezac, at the end of his rope and exhausted, swelled up like a toad and snapped at the interpreter, "Tell him in my opinion the Germans have gone to the Meuse to fish."

This collision of commanders fell into the lap of General Joffre. And while he was pondering it, he received a telegram from Sir John saying that the BEF was tired and that he was giving it a ten-day rest.

General Joffre tore himself away from pushing Plan 17 and drove to meet Sir John. The two liked each other at once. It was a relief for Sir John to talk to a calm, undismayed French leader who listened. Also, the testy Briton had simmered down and was ready to fight Germans: Lord Kitchener had come over from London to investigate and had laid down the law about cooperating with the French.

Joffre, back in his headquarters, called for goose

liver as bad news poured in. Frenchmen were being defeated in Alsace-Lorraine. Near Mons a nine-mile gap had developed on the right of the British army. When hordes of Germans butted straight at the Allies, Sir John ordered a retreat to save his army from being annihilated. He placed the blame for the mess squarely on Lanrezac.

During the retreat from Mons, the morale of the Tommies tumbled. Many of them were cut off and left in Belgium. They tried to rejoin their units, but failed because of the position of the German army.

When word of the retreat reached Joffre, he did not lose his head, although things looked alarming. He abandoned Plan 17 on the twenty-fifth of August 1914, and began transferring soldiers to the right wing, near Paris. Now his idea was to form a new army that could strike the west finger of the German claw.

Soon Papa Joffre astounded civilian leaders. He violated the divine doctrine of the attack and ordered a retreat all along the line that faced the German claw. Clemenceau, and other French politicians, felt that they should never have trusted the aloof, sphinx-like general in the first place. France looked doomed.

But General Joffre, more shrewd than his opponent, General von Moltke, moved about the fearful scene, learning, talking to his officers, talking to his soldiers — *"mes enfants"* he called them. Joffre never lost heart.

The timid Moltke didn't move anywhere. His headquarters, back on the beautiful Rhine River, one hundred and sixty miles from the battles, could easily have been on the moon. In addition, Belgians cut the telephone lines to the Front, and his generals had overly optimistic reports about the fighting delivered to him.

The turmoil on the French side was increased by the "new" generals. Joffre had dismissed dozens of senior leaders for failing to produce and replaced them with novices. On the twenty-fifth of September he sent for his friend Lanrezac. Their friendship was over. It was obvious now that Lanrezac lacked the character to be a great general. He had become indecisive, and he had given the idea to his staff officers that he was "washing his hands of the whole business." He was anxious that history record that the failure was Joffre's, not his.

"My comrade," Joffre said to Lanrezac, "you are finished. I hate to tell you this, but I have to."

Joffre's conference with Lanrezac's successor generated even fewer words. "Do you feel up to commanding an army?" Joffre asked Lanrezac's chief assistant, General Louis Franchet d'Esperey. When d'Esperey said yes, Joffre nodded, "Go ahead."

About this time, on the German side, Moltke worried because news from Russia was bad. Consequently, he threw a wrench into the invasion plan by taking soldiers from the west finger of the German claw and hurrying them by train across Europe to fight the Russian steamroller.

Then Moltke, timid and unsure, thought that his soldiers in France were covering too wide a front, so he weakened the German plan again by shifting that finger of the invasion to the east of Paris. Moltke was the best friend Papa Joffre had.

Nonetheless, Moltke's talons kept reaching south further and further into France. On August 31, 1914, a German plane flew over the capital, dropping leaflets warning: IN THREE DAYS, THE GERMANS WILL BE IN PARIS.

Streams of citizens left the city, crowding the road southeast to Tours. Confusion and fear exhausted the Parisians who remained. The government of France fled to Bordeaux. Barbed-wire entanglements went up in the streets of the most beautiful city in the world. Soldiers placed dynamite under the bridges so that they could be blown up to hinder the oncoming Germans. Even the huge sewers were barricaded.

It turned unbelievably hot. Papa Joffre reacted to the stifling weather by sitting quietly under an apple tree at his headquarters at Bar-sur-Aube, southeast of Paris, fanning his flushed red face and studying maps and reports. Occasionally, like an old fountain gushing water, he spouted an order.

Along the Marne River, French and British soldiers were giving their lives rather than let the Germans capture Paris. Sir John French grew timid, but Papa Joffre stiffened him. General Joseph Gallieni, the military governor of Paris, conceived a unique idea. He arranged for six thousand soldiers to be hauled to the Front in Paris taxicabs.

The fate of France was balancing on the scale. Finally Joffre brought more soldiers back from the northeast and created a new army to strike the German west flank. Then he fell ill. The pressure and long hours were too much.

The old general found himself almost the sole patient in a Paris hospital. Trains were shifting wounded
elsewhere. With doctors and nurses laboring to get him
well, Papa Joffre penned his Order of the Day and sent
it to the men of his armies:

WE ARE ENGAGED IN THE BATTLE ON WHICH DEPENDS
THE FUTURE OF OUR COUNTRY. . . . NO ONE MUST LOOK
BACK. TROOPS THAT CANNOT ADVANCE MUST HOLD THEIR
GROUND.

At the crucial moment in the Battle of the Marne,
one of the most important in history, Papa Joffre
ordered a counterattack. One of his great characteristics helped him: unshakable confidence. Generals in
contact with him felt buoyed up; they passed his self-
reliance down to their troops. Moltke lost his nerve
during the fierce fighting and ordered a retreat, mysti-
fying German soldiers. They had been winning, but
now, suddenly, they were ordered to fall back.

Joffre wrote later, "The German armies, on the
whole, had gone back in good order. . . . They were not
broken in spirit." He went on to describe a "race to
the sea" that ended with the enemies digging trenches
facing each other, extending from Nieuport on the
English Channel all the way to Switzerland.

Joffre was hailed as the hero of the Marne, but in
1915 he was confronted with a deadlock on the battlefield. He chased the illusion of victory, ordering
straight-ahead attacks that cost thousands of lives. In

June 1916, Joffre, believing that the British and French armies would win if they attacked in unison, selected the Somme as a battle area. It proved a huge slaughterhouse. In the same year, Joffre conceived the battle at Verdun that bled France white.

Joffre's political enemies rose in full cry, with the Tiger, Clemenceau, leading the pack. As a result, Joffre was retired in December 1916, in favor of the spellbinder who was to prove a failure, young General Robert Nivelle.

Joffre, now a marshal of France, sailed for the United States in April 1917, with Prime Minister Arthur Balfour of Britain and former Prime Minister René Vivani of France, to ask for loans to carry on the war. The trio was successful.

Joffre found the United States burning with war fever. On the day the distinguished visitors landed, a newspaper hailed him on its front page: HERO OF THE MARNE PEOPLE'S HERO.

Americans flocked to see him. Wherever he went herds of newsmen followed. He parried questions with dignity. He realized that the American army, although in the war, was not ready to fight, that its air force had only fifty-five planes, many of them obsolete. Nevertheless, Papa Joffre urged President Wilson to send a division to France as soon as possible. "It will help Allied morale," Joffre said.

Back in France, the old general found the air cooler. His enemies laughed because he hated to use the telephone. Clemenceau thought him an anachronism.

When the war ended in November 1918, Clemenceau, Premier of France once again, organized a parade to march up the Champs Elysées, under the Arch of Triumph, to celebrate the victory. In the excitement, he forgot to invite the Hero of the Marne. An aide hurried to the old marshal with an invitation to the reviewing stand and with an apology. Joffre said, "No apologies, dear sir. There are moments when one can't think of everybody."

EDITH CAVELL
Red Cross Nurse

EDITH CAVELL and a group of her nurses stood on the Post Road at the main entrance of the newly built, V-shaped nursing school in Brussels. Across the road two Germans in spiked helmets and gray uniforms, one a private, the other a sergeant, seemed symbolic of the plight that had overtaken the city.

The private held a black and white placard against the door of a tobacco shop and looked at his superior for approval. With Teutonic thoroughness, the cardboard sign was headed PLACARD.

The sergeant, on the driver's seat of a two-wheeled, horse-drawn cart, said, "Get it higher."

"Herr Sergeant, any higher and no one will read."

"Higher!" the sergeant commanded.

When the private stood on his tiptoes, arms stretched toward the roof, the sergeant snapped, "Nail!" The strokes of the hammer sounded ominously along the avenue.

The private hopped into the cart. The sergeant addressed the horse in German, slapped its rump with the reins, and the wagon rumbled away over the cobblestones.

The sign warned in French:

August 20, 1914
ANYONE   WHO   HARBORS   ENEMY   SOLDIERS
WILL BE SHOT.

It was signed by a German commander.

Miss Cavell stared. "I don't believe it," she said.

A nurse at her elbow snorted, "Don't you?" Then, making sure that she was not overheard, she whispered, "They are capable of anything. Anything, I tell you! They shoot captured *francs-tireurs* like wild dogs. Why? For defending their country. Not even a trial. These invaders put the torch to our towns. Don't trust them any more than you'd trust the Devil himself."

The black and white placard was literally the handwriting on the wall. Another nurse said, "Anyone who disobeys that has a foot in the grave."

Edith Cavell set her jaw. She had already harbored two British soldiers and had directed them to the Dutch border — men who had been cut off from their units and who were unable to return to them. Her eyes flashed. She was not going to change a whit from anything she conceived as her duty.

But back in her room at the nursing school, she felt

Edith Cavell. (United Press International Photo)

cold, even though the August breeze wafting through the window was warm. She soothed herself by talking to her two best friends, her mongrel dogs Jackie and Don. Nearby on an easel stood a half-finished still life in oil. She lifted a brush from a kerosene-filled tray and put it back. With such danger in Brussels, a human plague blighting life, she knew that she could never wet another brush until the war was over.

As if to reassure herself, she turned to her mirror. She was forty-nine, but there was not a streak of gray in her hair. She wore it swept back over a "rat," with a bun at the back. The high, stiff white collar of her navy-blue uniform lent dignity to her appearance. Her white nurse's cap, molded in the shape of a half crown, seemed a bit like an earth-made halo. She muttered at her own image, "It was my duty to help them."

The thought of duty comforted her. Her father, Frederick Cavell, rector in the idyllic village of Swardeston in eastern England, had drilled the meaning of duty into her since childhood. He was a stern man of slender means who never compromised. He continually harped on the word *duty*.

" 'Fear God and keep his commandments,' " he would quote to his family. " 'This is the whole duty of man.' It is a heaven-directed, moral obligation fastened on us by the Creator — to carry out laws, to revere Him, to honor our parents, to refrain from murdering and stealing, and to love our neighbors."

The Reverend Cavell's Church of England sermons could pack many meanings and connotations into the word *duty*. Around the table in the rectory with his wife and children it was the subject of daily discourse. Anyone who failed to do his duty was not only letting God and his country down, but was betraying himself. Edith imitated the zeal of her father at an early age by accepting the responsibility of caring for her two younger sisters and baby brother. She relished his praise.

Edith Cavell had not entered nursing for personal gain. By 1914 she had little to show for her years in the profession except a sapphire pendant. When she finished a tour as head nurse in an infirmary in the London slums, her staff had given it to her. Next to Jackie and Don, it was her most precious possession.

Cavell's practicable application of duty made her one of the best-known people in Brussels. She had come to the city in 1907 to nurse a sick child who was a patient of the eminent surgeon Dr. Antoine Depage. He was concerned over the poor state of nurses' training in Europe. Consequently, with the invaluable help of his cultured and socially prominent wife Marie and interested Belgians, he sponsored the nursing school L'Ecole Belge d'Infirmières. Edith Cavell stayed on in Brussels and assisted the doctor in his work. Now, in 1914, she ran the school efficiently. No one in Brussels was busier or more content — until the Germans came.

The townspeople were astonished that such a small woman — five feet three inches tall and about one hundred and ten pounds — could accomplish so much. Occasionally someone would rationalize, "Of course she does a lot. She works fourteen hours a day."

Although Cavell was devoted to her duty, she was far from subservient. Once Dr. Depage, in the clutches of a bad day, sent for her and demanded that a student nurse be dismissed.

"Why?" Miss Cavell wanted to know.

"She's wearing a soft collar."

"But, Dr. Depage, that's not grounds for dismissal."

"I don't care what you do. Never let me see her again."

Edith Cavell earned the admiration of her students and staff by saying, "Doctor, when you are in a reasonable state of mind, I'll be glad to talk about regulations with you."

But Edith Cavell was a woman with few friends, a person without humor, and with rigid ideas about nursing. This led her, at times, to difficulties with her staff. But there was never any misunderstanding about who ran the school.

Edith Cavell was determined to make each student into the best nurse possible. That was her sole aim in life. She disabused apprentices of the idea that nursing was romantic: cooling fevered brows under the direction of handsome doctors. There is some of that, she said, but she emphasized that nursing is hard, unattractive work. Her students soon learned that only the most dedicated could win her approval and the coveted nurse's diploma. She held that the apprentices must have the primary essentials of common sense and an even temperament, and not be easily confused or irritated. Cavell told her pupils that they must be quiet, neat, vigilant, and able to learn a system. She impressed on them that if they were to survive they must take care of their own health.

As for techniques, her students discovered that unless you have a real concern for people, learning the skills of the profession can be drudgery. The young nurses had to know how to make blood-letting leeches bite, how to prepare and heat a mustard plaster for a patient's chest, how to make up a bed for a patient who had bedsores, and so on. The list seemed endless.

When the Germans entered Brussels, Edith Cavell's work load increased. She still ran the school, but she converted part of it into a clinic for sick people. There was plenty to do. Numbers of citizens suffered from mental illness because of worries over the future of their country and of relatives who were in the fighting. Refugees were thronging into the city, most of them living in the streets without sanitary arrangements. Fortunately, few wounded soldiers were brought into Brussels; most of them were carried elsewhere.

The Germans added to the difficulties, even quartering soldiers in private homes. The German high command demanded huge quantities of food for its soldiers and levied a fine of fifty million francs on the city. Food stores shut down because of lack of supplies. Businesses closed.

The invaders were puzzled by the hatred they met. The *francs-tireurs* perplexed them. The Germans looked upon themselves as benevolent conquerors. They encouraged Brussels to go on with its normal life. They loved the Belgian children, gave them food, and at times let them crawl on the cannon. Why should their parents be unreceptive and sullen?

Two banners over the distraught city became symbolic. The flagpole at the townhall flew the black, red, and white banner of the invaders. From the nursing school hung the Red Cross flag, hallmark of hope. Edith Cavell had been given permission by the conquerors to run the school as a Red Cross hospital. It would care for the wounded and sick of all nationalities.

Brussels citizens, drawn together by adversity, felt like brothers. To irritate the Germans, they pretended not to see them, and placed American flags in shop windows. The Germans decided that they could do nothing about the first vexation, and although the flags galled them, they did not order them removed because America was neutral; it was best not to provoke her.

An additional worry plagued the Germans. After the battle at Mons on August 24, 1914, the British retreated into France, leaving several thousand soldiers stranded behind the German lines. Although many of these men were wounded and in wretched condition, the Germans wanted no force wandering around that might strengthen the *francs-tireurs*. And the invaders were extremely anxious that the stragglers not return to Britain, where they could be re-equipped and return to fight. Consequently, the Germans decided to hunt the stragglers down to the last man.

The first Edith Cavell knew about these unfortunate soldiers was when peasants passed the word into the city. They described incidents in the lives of the hunted men, telling how many of them were hiding in miners' huts and on small farms in the Forêt de Spignes, about six miles from Brussels. "The Germans search and search," the peasants said. "Last week they found thirteen *soldats anglais* in stacks of hay and shot them like rabbits."

People in the city also learned that the Prince and Princess de Croy, who owned a large part of the forest, were assisting the stragglers with the help of the peasants.

But it was dangerous to help stragglers. There was no problem in recognizing Germans when they donned civilian clothes, but extremely hard to detect traitors and informers; Belgians in the pay of the Germans caused great concern. It took daring and bravery for one to go against the orders of the conquerors.

Edith Cavell was tested one evening in November 1914. She was alone at her desk in the school after supper when a tall Belgian, standing in the dimly lit hall, knocked on her door and said, "May I come in, please? May I close the door?"

Miss Cavell took him to be a new patient. The man looked worried and gaunt.

The visitor began with no ceremony. "I need your help. Badly. I'm guiding a British colonel and a ser-

geant to the border. I have them camping out in the
street nearby, with refugees. But if I don't move them
soon the Germans may discover them in the street-by-
street, house-to-house search they're making."

Edith recoiled. Was this a trap? Through the window, the yellow light of a street lamp illuminated the
placard. She found her voice. "Who are you?"

The visitor disregarded the question. "If these men
are found — " he said. He clucked his lips and fired an
imaginary pistol against his forehead. He continued
quickly, "There's a ring of patriots helping these stragglers, such people as the architect Philippe Baucq and
the schoolteacher Mademoiselle Louise Thuliez."

Miss Cavell frowned. Why should this man disclose
names?

Then the stranger buoyed her confidence by blurting, "I'm Hermann Capiau, an engineer from a village
near Mons." He proved his identity and handed Edith
Cavell a note from the influential Madame Marie
Depage saying that he could be trusted. He finished, "I
helped these two Britishers up from Mons. All of us
riding in a coal wagon, past sentries and patrols, at the
risk of our lives. Please assist us, please!"

There was no question in Edith Cavell's mind where
her duty lay. At midnight, she opened the back door of
the hospital and Hermann Capiau led the two men
inside. Sergeant Meachim, husky and young, was in
good shape, but the colonel, old and weak, seemed on
the verge of a nervous breakdown. In the kitchen when
Edith gave them mugs of milk, the colonel burst into

tears and said he lacked the strength to go on. Sergeant Meachim cradled his arm around the older man's shoulders and comforted him as if he were an upset child.

Edith Cavell hid the two stragglers until they could proceed with the help of a guide.

The next involvement, in the late spring of 1915, produced even more hazards. A man only an inch or two taller than Miss Cavell walked into the school with the brave Belgian woman Mademoiselle Louise Thuliez. He smiled, bowed from the waist, and said, "Mademoiselle Cavell, permit me. I am Lieutenant Georges Gaston Quien, of the Eleventh Territorial Regiment of France." Mademoiselle Thuliez vouched for him and told how, as a volunteer, Lieutenant Quien had worked with her to guide Allied soldiers to the border. He had also assisted the de Croys. "I have an infected toe," he said. "I need help."

"Lieutenant" Quien neglected to say that he was a former jailbird whom the Germans had taken out of prison, and that he was paid by them to spy on people suspected of helping stragglers. Edith Cavell agreed to assist Georges Quien and admitted him to the hospital as a patient.

Nurse Cavell soon found herself more involved in the ring than formerly because both Monsieur Baucq and Prince de Croy had talked her into assisting additional stragglers. The prince, who looked like a professor, asked her to set up a "permanent" hiding place in the school, "because it's in the suburbs, and the police are watching the city." She agreed.

The situation heaped pressure on her. There was difficulty getting enough food for her patients, the nurses, and the fugitives. It was hard to control some of the stragglers; worn out by the strain of hiding, the soldiers resented being told what to do by a pint-sized, bossy woman.

Soon news from the border chilled her: the Germans were doubling their guards and were erecting miles of electrically charged barbed-wire fence. When they announced that they had captured a party of fugitives, Miss Cavell worried. Were they men she had sent? She received a "thank-you" note from a straggler who had reached London. What would have happened if that note had been intercepted?

Other nurses began to worry. Not all of them approved of Nurse Cavell's work in the ring, fearing that if it were discovered the Germans would close the school. Her friend Elisabeth Wilkins said, "I must tell you, Edith, you're becoming skittish and irritable." Dr. George Hostelet, himself in the ring, warned that there was talk around town that she was helping in the undercover work. "I urge you to pull out now," he said.   .

"I can't," Miss Cavell said. "More men are coming in, not only from Mons but from other battles. They need help."

Edith Cavell now found herself confronted by a conflict of duty. On the one hand stood her moral ob-

ligation to the nurses and the school, on the other her
duty to her fellowman and her country. She chose the
latter.

Shortly thereafter, Sister Wilkins became suspicious
of "Lieutenant" Quien. "This little man," she told
Miss Cavell, "does not seem real to me. He's too in-
quisitive." And she went on to say that she disliked his
ardor toward the young girls in training. "I suspect
him of everything low," Sister Wilkins said. "Please
throw Quien out and withdraw from your dangerous
work before it's too late."

Edith Cavell did make Mr. Quien leave, although he
protested that his toe still hurt. She countered by saying, "I cannot stand for you to demoralize my young
girls." Then, after Quien departed, Nurse Cavell told
Sister Wilkins that their duty was clear: aid to the
stragglers would continue.

Now, with the Brussels underground spreading details of the German tightening of their net, Prince de
Croy warned Edith Cavell that she was in danger, and
he suggested that she withdraw from the ring. Again
she said that it was her duty to continue. She appeared
on the verge of collapse, but when her senior nurses
told her to slow down she insisted that she had an
obligation to keep going.

In late August 1915, the German ax fell. Into the
school marched a file of German soldiers. They arrested Miss Cavell and Mademoiselle Thuliez and
placed them in a prison wagon called the "salad bas-
ket." In Saint-Gilles prison, the two women found

ringleader Philippe Baucq and Hermann Capiau in adjacent cells. Presently, German police brought in Sister Wilkins, but they released her and placed the nursing school under guard.

German officials took away Nurse Cavell's neat uniform and furnished her with drab prison garb. Questioning began — at length. They hammered at her that she would benefit if she admitted her obvious guilt in helping Allied soldiers.

The arrests caused a sensation. Brussels citizens demanded her immediate release.

When Mr. Brand Whitlock, the American minister in Brussels, heard of the action, he was shocked. He, too, demanded Miss Cavell's release, stating that he not only represented the United States, but Great Britain as well (Britain had no representative in Belgium at that time). The Germans refused.

Mr. Hugh Gibson, a hot-tempered and persuasive clerk in the American legation, teamed up with Maître Gaston de Leval, a lawyer employed by the legation, and with the Marqués de Villalobar, the Spanish minister to Belgium, to try to extricate Miss Cavell. They received no response from the Germans.

The diplomats repeatedly pressed for aid to Miss Cavell but without results. Finally, Baron von der Lancken, the German governor-general of Belgium, replied that because she had admitted her guilt she was now in solitary confinement and could not be interviewed.

Edith Cavell had become so exhausted by her regular work and her underground activities that she almost welcomed life in prison cell Number 23 because she could rest. In the next nine weeks she concentrated on reading her Bible. She did write occasional letters, some to the nurses. In one she said, "If Jackie is sad, tell him I will be back soon."

On the first day of her trial Edith Cavell stood with Philippe Baucq, Princess de Croy, and thirty-three others while the five German judges marched in. Infantrymen with spiked helmets, rifles, and fixed bayonets guarded the prisoners.

The treatment Edith Cavell had received since her arrest was a throwback to the Spanish Inquisition, when people were arrested suddenly, not informed of the charges against them, and not permitted to seek counsel. Only on entering the court was she permitted to meet her lawyer, Maître Sadi Kirschen. This able barrister was severely handicapped. He was forced to learn about her case only as it unfolded in court. The trial was held in a courtroom that was closed to all spectators except German officers. The record of the trial is fragmentary and tells little of the procedure.

Miss Cavell was remarkable in that she did not see her situation in the courtroom in terms of self-interest. As witness after witness testified against her, she saw the trial as a demonstration of the deep feelings of hatred the Germans possessed toward her countrymen.

Dr. Stöber, the prosecutor, adjusted his monocle and stared at the little woman in the witness chair. He said,

"Miss Cavell, from November 1914 to July 1915 you lodged French and English soldiers. One was a colonel. *Right?*"

"Yes," Edith Cavell said.

"You also helped Belgians of military age. You took them into your house and gave them money. Right?"

"Yes."

"Who was your chief? The Prince de Croy?"

"We had no chief. He was concerned only with sending us men. To some of them, he gave money."

"How many men have you helped to the frontier?"

"About two hundred."

"Why did you help them?"

"Because I am a patriot."

When a member of the court remarked that she had been foolish because the English she helped were ungrateful, Edith Cavell bristled, "They are not ungrateful! Some of them wrote and thanked me when they got to England."

Edith Cavell's lawyer stressed her invaluable aid to the nursing profession and reviewed her service to the people of Brussels. He finally asked her, "What have you to say against these charges? What can you say in your defense?"

Edith Cavell stunned him by blurting, "Nothing!"

She was an enigma. She seemed out to convict herself.

The trial droned on — toward the execution bullets. The nurses and the people of the city were worked up, eager to learn the verdicts. German officers, off duty, who had dropped in for the entertainment, would say nothing to the populace. No one could approach the members of the court.

On the fourth day the prisoners and their lawyers stood to receive the sentences. Stöber read from a paper, "Under paragraph fifty-eight of the German Military Code — the verdicts: Death for Prince de Croy. Death for Philippe Baucq, Louise Thuliez, and Edith Cavell. Hermann Capiau, fifteen years' confinement. The Princess de Croy, ten years' confinement." Other punishments varied from five to ten years' imprisonment.

Edith Cavell, perfectly composed, said to her lawyer, "There's no use appealing. They were out to convict me because I'm English."

Queen Mary of England did appeal on behalf of Edith Cavell, but it did no good. The same diplomats tried again, with the same results. Later, Americans criticized Mr. Whitlock's efforts. Some believed that although he was ill, he had not acted vigorously enough.

When the Marqués de Villalobar stepped in again, proposing that Baron von der Lancken phone the Kaiser for permission to void her sentence, the baron said, "The Kaiser would not dare to interfere with the findings of a military court."

On October 11, 1915, Mr. Whitlock was permitted to arrange for the Reverend Horace Gahan to give Miss Cavell Holy Communion. The two recited the words of the hymn "Abide with Me."

The next day at dawn Edith Cavell wrote in her prayer book:

Died at 7 A.M. *on October 12, 1915*
With Love to My Mother
E. Cavell

There is discussion about her last words. Probably they were, "Patriotism is not enough." No one can be certain of what she meant.

She was placed in an automobile that had its side curtains drawn. When the car pulled up at the Tir National rifle range, two hundred and fifty German infantrymen, rifles loaded and locked, waited for her and the other prisoners. She was taken out back, in front of the target butts, tied to a stake, and blindfolded. A detachment of the soldiers toed a line in the dirt, aimed, and fired.

Astonishment and horror spread over the world at the announcement of Edith Cavell's death. Millions saw in the action German militarism unmasked. The Kaiser was condemned in almost every country for failure to prevent her execution. Her death proved a boon to British recruiters because thousands of young men who had been holding back now volunteered to enlist.

Three years later, when King Albert rode his horse back into his capital, all Brussels greeted him. His first public act was to visit scenes associated with Edith Cavell's trial and death.

In May 1919, her body was exhumed and taken to

Westminster Abbey in London, where a huge crowd assembled to see her memory honored at a ceremony usually reserved for soldiers. She was buried in the cemetery of Norwich Cathedral, near her birthplace.

A statue of Edith Cavell stands near Trafalgar Square in the center of London. And in Brussels, to make sure that people remember the heroine who believed that duty to her fellowman was more important than life itself, an avenue bears her name and the nursing school has become known as the Institut Edith Cavell–Marie Depage.

5

FRITZ KREISLER
Violinist at War

FRITZ KREISLER was oblivious to the spectacular beauty of the rocky walls at Ragaz, Switzerland. The famous violinist's eyes had been glued to a newspaper column, datelined Vienna, July 31, 1914, ever since the hotel porter had delivered the paper to his room. Although his wife Harriet had already seen the paper, Kreisler read the headlines aloud, his low soft voice a note higher and crammed with tension: "Austria-Hungary Prepares for War. Third Austrian Army Corps Called to the Colors. Russia Readying Armies."

Kreisler knew that trouble was ahead for Austria, his country. In the involved political situation, the Russians would back the Serbs, enemies of the Austrians. This would result in Russia's fighting Austria.

It was simple for Harriet Kreisler to know how profoundly her husband felt. He had three loves: his wife, Austria, and his violin. His world was crashing.

The news threatened a startling career. Fritz Kreisler had been a child prodigy who could read music

Fritz Kreisler and his wife. (United Press International Photo)

before he could read words. At seven, wearing tight, black satin trousers and high tasseled boots, he played before audiences for a reward he liked: a box of candy. At ten, he won the Vienna Conservatory's gold medal. When he was eleven, crowds flocked to hear him in Boston and New York, and later in Chicago and the largest cities in Europe—even in Russia. He practiced long hours on his violin, yet when he grew older he rebelled at systematic drill, saying "a violinist plays with his mind and not as a result of practice."

Fritz Kreisler's life suddenly became more meaningful when, at the age of twenty-six, as he was sailing from America back to Europe, he fell in love. He was in the ship's barbershop having his hair cut when he saw a charming red-haired girl in the mirror. He could hardly wait to pay the barber. Then he dashed out to inquire who she was. He made it his business to meet her, and after a year's courtship he and Harriet Lies of New York City were married.

Both were Roman Catholics, and because Harriet was a divorcée their marriage was not recognized by the Church. Years later, however, the noted Monsignor Fulton J. Sheen blessed their union. There were unrevealed circumstances that made possible such a validation.

Kreisler's career blossomed with his wife's help. Herself a violinist and intensely interested in his amazing talent, she inspired him. He became a world-renowned artist. But now, with lights blinking out all over Europe, his career was unquestionably going to be affected.

Kreisler saw Austria-Hungary's future in doubt. Russia would certainly try to gobble up his country's land and people. What would happen if his country were defeated?

He told Harriet what she already sensed. He would leave the hot mineral baths at Ragaz on the first train, to rejoin his regiment. He had been a reserve officer in the Third Corps, although two years had passed since he resigned to devote himself entirely to the violin.

In spite of Kreisler's training, the thought that the lives of soldiers would now depend on his orders jarred him. He searched himself. Was he qualified for a position of such responsibility? A score of similar questions bothered him. He reviewed his situation and finally determined that he could and would lead men successfully in battle.

Kreisler turned to another aspect of his situation. Joining his regiment meant leaving Harriet and giving up the work he adored. He discussed every possible angle with her. He had talked over all problems with her throughout their married life. Now they tried to peer into the future together: how much ground would be lost to other violinists not in the war? There were no clear answers.

Harriet understood Austria's tug on her husband's heartstrings. He loved its culture and its people, and he would fight for what he loved. She had seen at first hand how hard he had worked when he was a reserve lieutenant in the army. Hating to be separated from him, she had on one occasion received permission to accompany him on maneuvers. She had hiked over country roads with him at the rear of his platoon in the Third Infantry Regiment, sat with him by crackling campfires on moonlit nights, and when rains drenched them, she voiced no complaint. Now, Harriet realized that she could not go into combat with him, but she would do the next best thing: she would volunteer as an Austrian Red Cross nurse.

While the Kreislers were packing to leave Switzerland, to face an unknown future, Kreisler received a telegram from his father, a physician and violinist in Vienna. It was a rehash of a telegram received from the Austro-Hungarian government, summoning Fritz to active duty with his former regiment.

The dual monarchy of Austria-Hungary was galvanized into action by the declaration of war. The nation embraced fifty-two million souls: Germans (Austrians), Magyars (Hungarians), Czechs and Slovaks, Poles, Ukrainians (Ruthenes), Slovenes, Croats, Italians, Rumanians, even Serbs, and people of eight other cultures. The mélange of peoples made the country difficult to govern. But it was a land of surprising stability and prosperity due to the devotion of its ruler: dignified, eighty-four-year-old Franz Joseph I, a dedicated man responsive to the needs of his subjects, and one who loved peace. He could speak every language represented in his empire, an accomplishment that endeared him to his subjects. Kreisler called him "a grandfather to all his people." (Fritz Kreisler himself could not only speak all these languages but also French, Latin, and Greek.)

The old Emperor had his dislikes: the gasoline engine, the telephone, the elevator, new customs, and the Kaiser. But with Europe going up in flames, as much as the Emperor hated war, he believed that his country's salvation depended upon its alliance with Germany — a lifeline against Russia. However, not all of his subjects disliked fighting. Many felt happy when, at the urging of the Kaiser, the Emperor declared war on Serbia. This would be an adventure, a chance to even old scores with the Serbs. (Conflict between the two nations had started over Serbia's export of pigs and was known as the Pig War.)

And the old Emperor had his likes. One of them was Kreisler, who often played for him. Kreisler wrote: "He would come to me after each performance, as simply as any child, and in a half-apologetic whisper he would ask me to play those simple little tunes he understood."

The orchestra of war was tuning up when Kreisler's train puffed into the railroad yards of Vienna on August first. Scores of other trains, crammed with young soldiers, rolled out of the city. Thousands of Viennese were frantic with joy. The war had given each of them a feeling of exhilaration, a delirious sensation of being free, of being a hero girding himself to slay ancient enemies. On the streets, total strangers embraced at the slightest excuse. People sang patriotic songs in restaurants and in the streets. Kreisler had neither time nor inclination to celebrate. He had come to tell his father good-bye.

Fritz and Harriet found the same feelings in the streets of Leoben, near Graz, where he reported to the colonel of his regiment. The world seemed mad. People celebrated as if there were no tomorrow.

It was a happy week in Leoben while his Austrian regiment was assembling and being equipped. Fritz looked even more manly in his gray field uniform. He was a handsome six-footer, with surprisingly large hands for a violinist, a black mustache and a broad forehead that signaled virility and intelligence. He posed for a photo with Harriet, his hand on his sword. Harriet, almost as tall, seemed in her white Red Cross uniform as young as when he had first met her fourteen years ago.

On the afternoon before the regiment entrained for a combat zone, Kreisler poured hot water over his hands and wrists backstage in the auditorium in Leoben — a ritual that readied him for a performance. Officers, soldiers, their wives, and townspeople had packed the building to hear him. The aged colonel down in front, a grandnephew of the Emperor, and other officers propped their swords between their knees. The senior officer and a few other older people wore black armbands, in mourning for young Archduke Ferdinand and his wife, whose tragic deaths by pistol bullets from a Serbian "Black Hand" assassin had supplied the spark that had ignited the war.

Kreisler, in uniform, played "Humoresque," a piece

he had adapted for the violin. Tears came to people's eyes. In his music there was a hint of gypsy romance and rhythm, a vibrant quality, and pathos so real the notes seemed alive. He made the violin sing. The music bore into the heart of each listener as if the artist were playing solely for him. Even with war about to change the life of everyone in the audience, he made his listeners concentrate on the magic of his music.

After dinner the clock raced, with both man and wife dreading the moment of parting. When the time came to say good-bye, he took his wife in his arms. The best he could do was, "I'll be back."

"I know you will," she said. "I'll be waiting. Send me word of your health every chance you get. I'm proud of you."

When Lieutenant Kreisler was asked later how he felt when leaving Leoben, he said, "I was but a cog in a great wheel—an atom in that great mass." On the troop train the men were packed like small fish in a tin can. No one in the lieutenants' car knew the train's destination. Two days later, when the engine was snorting and wheezing as it pulled its rattling and creaking coaches through the wild Carpathian Mountains, the colonel sent his adjutant to the junior officers with the message, "Gentlemen, we detrain shortly in eastern Galicia at Strij, south of the fortress of Lemberg."

About three thousand Austro-Hungarian soldiers joined them when the engine puffed to a stop, and then the march started.

Kreisler had never been in a more lonely land. It

was a mountainous country where villagers toiled from daylight till dark to raise crops in worn-out soil, a land where temperatures plummeted to forty below in winter. Now the August sun cooked the men as they slouched along, the straps of their fifty-five-pound packs and their rifles biting into their shoulders.

The roads, most of them below the level of the dull-brown fields, lay ankle deep in dust. Great clouds of it choked the soldiers. The column spread out in spite of orders from the colonel to close up. He rode a horse in the gap between the advance guard and the main body, where he could breathe. Just behind him a horseman bore the proud black-and-yellow regimental colors. Lieutenant Kreisler's platoon of fifty-five men, two buglers, and four first-aid men, trekked in the main body. None except the colonel knew where they were going. A rumor ran through the long line, "We're headed for the border to keep the Russians from entering the country."

The column of almost seven thousand men toiled through wretched villages. The huts, some of wood, some of stone, some red, some blue, leaned on each other. Almost every door bore a crucifix. Close by stood manure piles. Naked babies played in the dirt streets. Barefooted women in voluminous skirts reaching to their ankles appeared in the doorways to watch the soldiers. Some of the women wore wooden rings as ornaments around their heads, while others had covered their hair with polka-dotted cloths. The soldiers passed oxen and dogs yoked to plows and carts, tended by tired-looking men with high cheekbones. There was one inspiring sight: the Carpathian Mountains that rose behind them.

The men hiked on and on, away from the misty, snow-covered peaks, the dark wooded slopes, and the perpendicular cliffs. The Carpathians appeared unreal, like stage scenery. And there was a certain witchery: no matter how far the soldiers hiked, the mountains seemed to remain at the same distance. The marchers felt as if they were on a treadmill.

The twenty-two-mile hike on the first day exhausted large numbers of the soldiers; many had joined the colors from occupations that required little physical effort. But after the steaming rolling kitchens were tugged up by horses and everyone had been fed, the soldiers gathered around campfires to drink coffee and sing. The cedar forest began to seem like a second home. Overhead a canopy of stars twinkled. Kreisler said that he stretched out beside a campfire, "my cape for a cover, my soul filled with exultation and happiness over the beauty about me."

The beauty vanished suddenly at four the next morning when a distant rumbling woke the camp. Shortly, the campers realized that the thunder was the sound of a cannonade. They were amazed. They had not expected to hear from the Russians for at least another hundred miles. Kreisler and his comrades could not know that the Czar had mobilized his armies faster than foreigners had believed possible.

When the hike toward the barking guns began, a

horseman trotted up to the colonel, saluted, and delivered a message. Then the colonel quickly assembled all the officers. "Gentlemen," he said, "accept my congratulations. I have good news for you. We may meet the enemy today, and I sincerely hope to lead you to the fight before evening." The colonel went on to say that other Austrian columns were heading for the fight on nearby parallel roads.

When the officers ran back with the news, the soldiers brandished their rifles toward the sky and yelled. They would run the Russians out of Galicia. In the excitement, all signs of fatigue vanished. Lieutenant Kreisler gave the command to his platoon, "With ball cartridges, load!"

During the regiment's advance, Russian shells burst with loud cracks at treetop height, covering many of the squads with a cone-shaped spray of shrapnel: lead balls almost a half-inch in diameter. The vicious pellets tore into the men as if they had been fired from shotguns at close range. A man near Kreisler fell dead, his eyes remaining open. Kreisler never forgot the horrible look on the soldier's face. Close by, wounded men screamed as they crumpled into the dirt. A four-engine Russki Vitiaz (Russian Knight) biplane droned over the Austrians. The soldiers fired at it but failed to bring it down.

Austro-Hungarian artillery, far to the rear, opened up in counter–battery fire, hoping to quiet the Russian cannon. Not being able to fire their weapons at the enemy shooting at them gave the Austrian infantry a futile feeling. Orders came from the colonel to dig trenches and telling them where to shovel.

The next day, when the colonel ordered his soldiers to leave their trenches and attack, enemy shells roared over. Fritz Kreisler noticed that, because of his acute hearing, he could not only tell the difference between Russian and Austrian shells, but that the enemy shells had a distinct sound when they zoomed to the summit of their trajectories. He reasoned that this peak was reached exactly halfway between the Russian artillery and the point of impact. He passed his discovery back to the Austrians' heavy guns, and for a few days he was employed as a valuable, one-man sound-ranging service that enabled the Austrian artillery to fire with deadly accuracy at the Russian guns.

Kreisler was back with his platoon when part of his regiment executed a wide sweep that bagged two hundred and forty Russian soldiers. Presently, he commanded a guard that escorted the Russians to the rear area. With such a number of prisoners, the Austrians appeared to be winning, but after Kreisler returned, an Austrian scout plane dropped a message with the black news that approximately five Russian army corps were coming.

The Austrians prepared for the invasion. They dug trenches again, erected barbed-wire fences in front of them as protection, and measured distances to various parts of the terrain, marking them with barrels of hay so that each rifleman could set his sights accurately when the showdown came.

During the work, the colonel assembled his officers. He looked years older. "Gentlemen," he said, "I'm happy to tell you that we're being strengthened soon by another corps. The enemy will still outnumber us, but we are determined defenders. Remember, it's our sworn duty to the Emperor to block the Russians." He tugged at his scraggy white beard as if he was uncertain what to say next. He ended the meeting by blurting, "Thank you. That's all."

Something about the colonel's voice or manner unsettled Fritz Kreisler. As he walked back to his trench, he tried to put on the best face possible, but his men appeared to have received the news by some eerie wireless. Most of them were writing last letters home.

The next morning at ten the Russians saluted the Austrians with white bursts from their artillery. Again shrapnel took its toll, while overhead the Russian Knight flew in circles. The Austrian soldiers in the trenches fired at it and yelled, "Get it down!" as if their officers could do this by some magic. The soldiers had the right idea, because after the plane dropped a few thirty-pound bombs, it flew back to the Russian artillery to drop messages to help the gunners. (Radio communication had not been developed to the extent where pilots could talk to men on the ground.)

Now Kreisler's field glasses let him pick up a dark blotch moving rapidly along the horizon. "Cavalry coming!" he shouted. His men grinned and fingered their rifles. It would be infantry against horsemen, with barbed-wire fences to stop the horses. But the cavalry screen parted, exposing masses of oncoming Russian foot soldiers. The battle opened with artillery on both sides firing as fast as possible.

The Austrians slew unbelievable numbers of Russians, but still more and more attacked. By nightfall the scene was horrible. A moonrise let the Austrians see Russian dead stacked along the barbed wire like cordwood. Kreisler wrote in his *Four Weeks in the Trenches*, "The bodies seemed like a monstrous sacrificial offering immolated on the altar of some fiendishly cruel, antique deity. I felt sick at heart and near swooning away."

Not even the colonel knew the extent of the fighting. There had been a head-on collision between three Austro-Hungarian armies and four Russian ones, along a two-hundred-mile front. In the next ten days hordes of Russians swept the Austro-Hungarians back. Kreisler's tired men couldn't believe it. "Why," they asked, "are we retreating when we stopped the Russians?"

Lieutenant Kreisler explained that there is more to a battle than one local area, but his men shook their heads as they plodded back toward the Carpathians.

During the retreat toward the mountains, Austro-Hungarian morale tumbled. Sheets of rain added to the gloom. Distribution of ammunition and food became a serious problem. The colonel had ordered it stacked in empty huts along the route, huts that had been abandoned by the peasants. But some soldiers took more food than they needed so that others starved. To get water, Kreisler's men drank from mud puddles. He said that he licked the grass in order to wet his tongue with the dew.

When Kreisler's platoon was placed in the rear guard, his troubles increased. Now, to slow down the Russians, his men occupied successive high points along the route, while the regiment hiked away. Kreisler sent his scouts to explore ravines, so that when he was forced to withdraw, to avoid having the platoon captured, he could do so without suffering a hail of Russian bullets.

Waiting on a lonely hill for the Russians was like waiting for a herd of executioners. When Kreisler's men opened fire, the Cossacks in the Russian advance guard knew what the best ploy was: they galloped around Kreisler's platoon to cut it off.

Pressure weighed on Kreisler. In the hard fighting his men were being killed and wounded. At each position the same problem bored into him: how long could he remain without being cut off? When he believed that his platoon could stay no longer, he ordered his soldiers to withdraw along the routes his scouts recommended, while another Austrian unit farther back furnished protection.

The problem of what to do with the wounded racked Kreisler. No ambulances accompanied this part of the rear guard. The broken, battered men could not be left to the "mercy" of the Russians, so they had to be lifted and carried in the arms of their comrades. It was pitiful, and extremely hard on the carriers. Meanwhile, Cossacks galloped in to try to wipe out Kreisler's platoon. By the time the retreat ended on September 6, 1914, only thirty-four men remained out of sixty-one, and the weary, downcast Austro-Hungarians dug in on the best ground they could find after backpedaling well over one hundred miles.

Up came the Russians in attack formation, but after scouting their enemies they, too, dug trenches, and for a while a stalemate existed. During this impasse a huge Russian private, with a red, chest-long beard, walked along the top of his trench, gesticulating. Kreisler's men wanted to shoot him — but they hesitated. They began to admire the clownish giant. And after a while an Austrian volunteer went out to talk to him. When they met halfway between the trenches they shook hands and traded tobacco. During the lull two Russians came to the Austrian trenches under a white flag to beg, in broken French, for food. Kreisler served as interpreter. He saw that the enemy soldiers were just as tired, just as dirty, and just as exhausted as his own men. Kreisler learned a fact of war: seldom do soldiers of warring nations hate each other; intense dislike is a mark of people in areas far removed from the battle-fields.

With more rain, the Austrian trenches, in low ground southwest of Lemberg, looked like irrigation ditches. For four days Kreisler and his men stood in stinking water. Fritz sighed with relief when orders arrived at midnight for his platoon to withdraw further. Perhaps a stream could be found in the morning where all could take baths. Kreisler had not had his clothes off in almost three weeks. He was also worried because his men were low in ammunition.

In the darkness, when Kreisler led his men out of the trench, he heard a thundering of hooves. Daring Cossacks were staging a most unorthodox attack, a cavalry charge in the dark. The clash was a hideous moment for men and animals.

Lieutenant Fritz Kreisler shot the horseman who rode him down firing a pistol at him. Then Kreisler fell, unconscious from almost unbearable pain in his shoulder and thigh.

Kreisler's life was saved by a faithful orderly who eventually got him to a horse-drawn ambulance — a torture bed on wheels. The hospital train was almost as rough, as it chugged and jerked toward Vienna. When it finally wheezed into the station, the wounded were greeted by teams of doctors and nurses. Among them stood Harriet.

As sick as Kreisler was, he felt better when he met his wife. After he had recuperated enough to go out, he saw that Vienna was a mess. The city was crowded with refugees from the Russians, and trains were bringing in thousands and thousands of wounded. When the hospitals and public buildings overflowed, the people of Vienna took the battered soldiers into their homes. A fuel shortage gripped the city. No longer was there singing in the streets.

The defeat around Lemberg was a severe blow to Austria-Hungary. The Russians first announced that they had captured two hundred thousand of its soldiers, then they reduced this estimate to seventy thousand and finally toned it down to ten thousand. No one can be sure how many soldiers trudged into Russia to be "guests of the Czar." The country of Franz Joseph lost Lemberg, its two hundred thousand people, plus about twenty thousand square miles of territory, including valuable oil fields.

Harriet cared for her husband for three weeks, and during this time his doctors stopped the rumor printed in many papers: "Fritz Kreisler, famous violinist, killed in action." With Harriet as special nurse, he moved to Carlsbad, Austria, a health resort. In a few weeks he was once again in civilian clothing; the doctors had declared him unfit for more military service. He felt relieved to be out of the war but despondent over leaving his comrades.

Kreisler found that he could use his shoulder (although he walked with a slight limp) so he proceeded with his musical career. Public interest in him was still high. The Boston *Herald* said that there had been more bulletins about his wounds than there had been notices about "General Joffre, General Sir John French, or any commanding officer in the German, Austrian, or Russian army."

As soon as he could, Kreisler and his wife sailed for the United States to pursue his profession. This was in December of 1914. He discovered that, while most Americans' sympathies lay with the Allies, his music was well received. He played in many benefits, specializing in those that helped children.

However, as 1917 approached, some American audiences hooted and booed him because he had been an Austrian officer. He was hurt by their intolerance. The chivalry in Galician trenches did not exist in every American city. War fever gripped the United States, and almost everything Germanic, or Austrian, was hated.

Kreisler issued a long statement which the New York *Times* printed. It described his service to his fatherland and told how he felt it his duty to serve his Emperor, and gave his feelings about accusations that were hurled at him. He acknowledged his love for America and the kindnesses he had received.

With fanatical hatred pitted against him he decided to quit the concert stage. He gave up $85,000 in contracts and retired with Harriet to the rocky coast of Maine at Seal Harbor.

A year after the war Kreisler left Maine to make a comeback in New York City. Although the Austro-Hungarian Empire no longer existed, he announced that he was playing for the Vienna Children's Milk Fund. He received an ovation. It was one of the great moments in a great career.

Kreisler's tours continued — with success. London gave him an unparalleled reception, as did another "enemy city," Paris. "Fritz Kreisler did not play the violin, he became the violin," Bruno Walter, the famous conductor, said later.

But the career of the brilliant violinist did not always run smoothly. In 1935 Kreisler revealed that he was the author of a large number of compositions for the violin that for long years had been published as the works of classical masters. Some musicians became angry, some became confused, but most of them, as well as music lovers, laughed and applauded. Kreisler said that he had indulged in the hoax to avoid seeing his name repeated endlessly as the composer.

The "Kreisler hoax," as it was called, was insignificant in his mind compared to what he saw developing in Berlin, where he owned a home. He now refused to play in Germany because of the persecution of the Jews. To escape from Hitler and his Nazi regime, the Kreislers took up residence in France in 1939. There the government promptly made him a commander of the Legion of Honor.

Kreisler eventually moved to the United States, a country he loved, and in 1943 he held up his hand to receive the oath to become a citizen. A few months later bad luck literally struck him while crossing Madison Avenue, in New York City. He was knocked down by a truck and suffered a fractured skull, internal injuries, and a rare form of amnesia. In the hospital, he could remember only parts of his life, and he could speak and understand nothing but Latin and Greek. Poor Harriet, at her wit's end, could not converse with the man she loved. But when he recovered his language facility, as he eventually did, there was the question: Did he remember how to play the violin?

To answer the fearful query, Harriet brought her own violin to his hospital room. She said, "Fritz, I'm

having trouble playing a passage from the Mendels-
sohn Violin Concerto. I forgot to bring the music. Will
you play it for me?"

"Of course," he said. He did, and with his old warm
touch.

Kreisler's success as one of the greatest musical interpreters and musicians of all time lay not only in his
astounding ability to write and play fresh, charming,
vibrant music, but also in his warm personality. He
died in 1962, almost eighty-eight. Harriet survived
him.

Once at a birthday party in his honor at the Ritz-
Carlton Hotel in New York, a party attended by hundreds of fans, Fritz Kreisler blew out a flock of candles
on a huge birthday cake. He said he would make no
speeches "because anything I said would sound like an
obituary." He concluded with a remark that had always amused him: "Harriet said that I could have been
a great musician if I had only practiced."

6

WINSTON CHURCHILL
The English Bulldog

ON THE EGYPTIAN DESERT, one hundred and fifty yards away from the British Twenty-first Lancers, stood a crowd of howling dervishes, Moslems in revolt. Most of them lacked guns. They carried swords, battle-axes, daggers, and sharp-pointed javelins. The few who owned Remington rifles fired shots at the British cavalry. The Moslems felt certain that they would gain victory.

The British colonel drew his sword, turned in his saddle, and spoke to his trumpeter. In quick succession, he blew trot, right wheel into line, and then charge. The horses, who knew the bugle calls as well as the troopers, raced across the sands toward the dervishes.

Lieutenant Winston Churchill, twenty-three years old, galloped to the front of his troop. The wind tore at his face. The hooves of the horses behind him beat a tattoo on the sand that sounded like distant thunder. Churchill, bending close to the neck of his pony, thrust his sword as far forward as he could reach, in approved style, beyond the animal's nose. Then, thinking of his injured shoulder, he sheathed his cutlass and whipped out his pistol.

In the collision, men on both sides fell dead and wounded. Horses screamed. Some animals toppled over, never to rise, while others, without riders, bucked away.

Churchill said afterwards, "I shot five dervishes. Two others were doubtful." Fortunately, he came through uninjured in this defeat of the Moslems in 1897.

That night in his tent, while his comrades rested, Winston Churchill put aside thoughts of the risk he had taken and the memory of dead and wounded Lancers so that he could write a letter about the charge for a London newspaper. He was an officer in the British army but was also serving as a war correspondent.

Such an exciting assignment was far more to his liking than schoolwork had been. As a fourteen-year-old, undersized boy at Harrow, he had disliked his studies. "I hated Latin, especially," he said. "My teacher called it a dead language. Nothing could have been more descriptive." And nothing could have been more lifeless than the Latin examination paper lying on Churchill's desk in the bleak Harrow classroom in 1888. In two hours of daydreaming, this small but sturdy boy with the thin, carrot-red hair and blue eyes had written only his name.

Winston Churchill exasperated his teachers, and some thought him an enigma. At Harrow he was one

Winston Churchill in the uniform of the First Lord of the Admiralty. (United Press International Photo)

of the worst students, especially pathetic in Latin, Greek, and arithmetic. He said that in arithmetic the numbers jumbled themselves up with little reason. For instance, he pointed out that in subtraction they borrowed from each other at the slightest excuse and demanded that they be paid back.

He wrote well for his age, but the teachers hounded him to use the dictionary. He said that that book was almost as puzzling as math. You had to keep turning the pages back and forth, looking up words that were hiding out. His teachers were astounded at his memory when he recited without error twelve hundred words of Macaulay's *Lays of Ancient Rome*. And with little trouble he memorized large portions of Bartlett's *Familiar Quotations*. However, when he recited he did not show off well because he lisped. Churchill improved his knowledge by reading. He said, "I liked best *Treasure Island* and books on history and war."

Teachers thought him as obstinate as a bulldog. Once, in another school, he had to report to the headmaster because he had broken several rules. The senior master frowned and said, "Churchill, I have very serious reason to be displeased with you."

Churchill, never awed by anyone, shot back, "And I, sir, have reasons equally serious to be displeased with you." The headmaster was so surprised that he did not punish Winston. The boy was impudent, but there was never any doubt about where he stood on matters.

One of his schoolmates said, "Winston broke almost every rule and was quite incorrigible." It was understandable that, in a day when whipping in schools was common, he was often flogged. The story goes that Churchill earned a whipping at St. George's School, at Ascot, because he could not manage his temper and had kicked the headmaster's straw hat to pieces. He was impatient, and he held on to that characteristic throughout this life.

Churchill talked incessantly, perhaps because he was lonesome. His father, Lord Randolph, a brilliant political leader, kept him at arm's length, recoiling when his son displayed affection. Being rejected was a bitter experience for the boy. His mother, who was the daughter of a prominent American businessman, was beautiful but at times aloof. Young Churchill said he looked at her as if she were some far-off fairy princess. He adored his understanding nurse, Mrs. Everest, and carried his troubles to her. When he grew up and had an office, he kept her picture in a prominent place.

When the time came for Winston to leave Harrow and strike out on his own, he did not go to a university but applied for the eighteen-month course at the Royal Military College at Sandhurst. But the entrance examinations were puzzles. He failed. One of his great characteristics now came to the fore: he refused to give up.

Churchill entered a cram school, and after overtime work, he squeezed into Sandhurst on the third try. Here he found work that he liked, and in 1895 he graduated eighth in a class of one hundred and fifty, receiving a commission as a lieutenant in the British

army with orders to report for duty to the colonel of
the Fourth Hussars stationed at Aldershot, not far
from London. Churchill enjoyed stalking about town,
on his time off, in his new, gaudy, blue-and-gold full-
dress uniform.

But life in the Fourth Hussars soon took on aspects
of life in a squirrel cage. Parade-ground drills, over
and over. Spit-and-polish inspections. Maneuvers, on
which flags represented the enemy. Boring. Churchill
itched to overcome real enemies.

By now he was reading everything he could get his
hands on, from Gibbon's *Decline and Fall of the
Roman Empire* to newspapers and magazines. He studied how writers expressed themselves and presented
their topics. Writing interested him. Because of the
"inhospitable regions of examinations at Harrow," as
he termed the tests, he had received three times the
average grounding in English. He said, "I thus [had
in] my bones the essential structure of the ordinary
British sentence—which is a noble thing."

In order to combine his two desires: experiencing
battle and obtaining assignments to write, Churchill
took leave from the army and worked as a war correspondent for London newspapers in Cuba, India,
and Egypt, and during the Boer War in South Africa.
These experiences led to his writing books, and before
putting up his pen in old age he had one hundred sixty
books and over eight hundred press articles to his
credit.

Churchill's writing was outstanding. Here he is at

twenty-four, as a war correspondent, writing about the
river Nile:

*It is the great waterway of Africa. It is the life
and soul of Egypt. It is Egypt, since without it
there is only desert. We shall drink its waters,
duly filtered. We shall continue to wash in it,
charged as it is with the magic mud which can
make the wilderness a garden and raise cities from
the desolate sand. On its waters we shall be carried
southwards to the war and on to Khartoum. It is
the cause of the war. It is the means by which we
fight. It is the end at which we aim. Through
every page which I write to you about the campaign your imagination must make the Nile flow.
It must glisten through the palm trees during the
actions. You must think of the lines of animals,
camels, horses and slaughter cattle, that march
from camps every evening to be watered. Without
the river we should never have started. Without
it we could not exist. Without it we can never return. . . . It will presently carry this letter to you.*

Certainly, not all of his prose was as poetic. For instance, he lashed out when he thought he had to, criti-
cizing Lord Kitchener, Sirdar of the British army in
Egypt, when that general ordered the tomb of a native
leader desecrated and the corpse's head cut off.

Churchill's work as a war correspondent led him in
and out of combat. A superb horseman, he was one of
the best polo players in the army.

In 1899, while in South Africa covering the Boer War for the London *Morning Post* at £250 a month and expenses, Winston Churchill was captured and thrown into a Boer prison camp. All prisoners dream of escaping, but few risk trying. Guards were posted not only around the camp but on the inside. Nevertheless, Churchill freed himself in a hair-raising adventure. He obtained a suit of civilian clothes and climbed to the roof of the lavatory; when the sentry was not looking, he dropped to the ground outside the wall. Next, he stole a three-hundred-mile ride through enemy country in the coal car of a train. His captors made a vigorous effort to catch him. They dispatched telegrams to likely points, offering "£25 for Winston Churchill, dead or alive." A very meager sum, and to his disgust one description said that he lisped. But Churchill not only escaped; he made money writing about his experiences.

When the back of the Boer resistance was broken in 1900, Churchill sailed back to London to find himself popular and something of a hero. Telegrams of congratulations poured in from all parts of the world.

He decided that his best course, toward helping England and himself, lay in politics, with writing as a sideline. Even though he was well known, he found the political arena rough. After ups and downs, he entered the House of Commons to represent the people of his area.

When he was thirty-three, he married the attractive Miss Clementine Hozier. It was a "small" wedding with sixteen hundred guests; the King and Queen sent presents.

Churchill did not always find life rewarding and pleasant. Suffragettes, who were members of the women's liberation movement of that time, opposed him in the belief that he was their enemy. They threw rotten eggs at him, and one even horsewhipped him. They thought—mistakenly—that he had said they should be whipped. With characteristic combativeness he fought back by opposing their movement vigorously.

Churchill's work in politics paid dividends when, in 1911, Prime Minister Herbert Asquith appointed him First Lord of the Admiralty with cabinet rank—the head of the navy. Churchill soared into the clouds with delight. One of the prerogatives of his office was the use of the beautiful seagoing yacht *Enchantress*, which carried a crew of almost one hundred. When he departed on cruises and inspection trips aboard her, he wore a navy-blue blazer sporting two rows of brass buttons, a winged collar with bow tie, blue trousers, and white shoes, all topped by a salty chief petty officer's cap. He loved life on the ocean wave and enjoyed telling the captain where to go. His friend Violet Asquith, daughter of the Prime Minister, summed up his attitude toward his new position: "His imagination was fired by the great ships that had now been entrusted to his keeping."

Up to then, Churchill had never wanted a big navy for Britain, but now that he was the head of it he worked to enlarge it.

Not everyone thought Churchill's appointment wise. Some believed him unpredictable and impetuous. His enemies labeled him a medal snatcher and a glory hunter. Some said, "Outside of being a brave soldier and a splendid writer, what special qualifications does he have? He talks too much." (On a quick lecture tour in the United States, under the auspices of Mark Twain, Churchill had talked the humorist down.) And Churchill irritated senior naval officers because of his habit of asking junior officers what they thought of their superiors. But he had friends at the top of British politics. They encountered the criticisms by saying that he was a resourceful, indefatigable worker who could improvise. He was indeed that.

Senior naval officers wondered how old Lord Fisher viewed the appointment. Fisher, a retired, crusty character of great prestige, had been First Sea Lord, the highest British naval officer. In 1904 he found the British navy in a sad state, on a par with the notoriously shabby Russian navy. For six years Fisher toiled to improve Britain's fleet, but he was only partially successful. He was opinionated, and the years had sharpened his tongue. Now living in Switzerland, he passed the word privately to friends that he suspected Churchill of working behind the scenes to oust Mr. Reginald McKenna from the position of First Lord (the senior member of the Admiralty) so that Churchill himself could have the post.

Churchill, who knew nothing of this slander by a man he counted as a friend, worked in his new position at the Admiralty like a person who had but a few hours to live and much to accomplish. He wore out secretaries with continuous dictation and spat out orders like bullets from a machine gun. Sometimes he kept his aides at his office until two in the morning, an hour that often saw him rise from his desk to demand brandy and chicken sandwiches.

Because of his work and unusual foresight, Churchill was among the handful in 1911 who saw that Germany and Britain would fight. To ready the navy, Churchill worked furiously, bettering its organization, moving admirals around, and retiring those he believed incompetent. Word sped about the fleet, "Winnie is knocking over admirals like ninepins." He plunged on, using every possible political contact to secure bigger guns, speedier ships, and improved plans to hurry up aviation.

But when war broke out, in spite of Churchill's and Fisher's efforts, the British navy was not thoroughly trained. Fortunately, the German navy helped out by being timid, staying in harbors and the Baltic Sea. There was, at first, only minor warfare. When dismal reports filtered back to Britain from the ill-equipped Royal Naval Division fighting near Antwerp, Churchill felt ill. He was battling papers instead of Germans. He despised his desk. He decided to go to Antwerp, but to get there he first had to secure permission from Lord Kitchener, head of the army. This seemed almost impossible.

"Lord K" was formidable, in character and force

head and shoulders over the army officers whom he controlled. He and Churchill had been antagonistic toward each other during the years Churchill had served as a war correspondent. Churchill thought him stern and ruthless, but he confronted him, bursting into Lord K's bedroom in the dead of night, blurting, "Sir, I want your permission to go to Antwerp and command our naval division." The old Lord looked across the years at the intruder and understood. He gave his approval, and Winston Churchill was off to battle as a commander of ground troops.

When Churchill arrived in Antwerp he found more chaos than he had expected. He discovered that he could not dash to the front lines and save the situation like a knight of the Middle Ages. Refugees thronged the city, camping in the streets. An artillery duel shook houses on the outskirts. Overhead, a zeppelin sounded its soft *whirr-whirr*, as it dropped bombs onto homes. The city was filled with columns of smoke and debris.

One thing was obvious to Churchill: Antwerp would have to surrender. He heartened his eight thousand sailors and Marines of the Royal Naval Division. Many of them became lost, but they helped Belgian soldiers slow down the invaders and secure French seaports that would have been gobbled up by the Germans.

When word spread in England that the First Lord of the Admiralty had rushed off to Antwerp to fight as a soldier, disillusionment set in. The British press, not knowing how Churchill's leadership in the naval brigade was helping to save French seaports, attacked him bitterly, calling his rush to Antwerp "immature." Many Britons agreed with the newspapers.

After the city fell, Churchill, uncaring for the press and public opinion, told Prime Minister Asquith, "I feel like a tiger. I want permission to stay in France permanently and lead these ground soldiers away from the obsolete tactics of twenty-five years ago. Are there not more alternatives than sending our armies to chew barbed wire in Flanders?"

Asquith replied, "Appreciate your feelings, but we can't spare you from the Navy." It took both Lord K and Asquith to get Churchill back to his desk at the Admiralty, but it wasn't easy.

Shortly after Churchill's return he heard that Colonel Ernest D. Swinton, and others, had an idea for a "land battleship." It would carry machine guns behind bullet-proof armor and would move on caterpillar tracks instead of wheels. Swinton was convinced that the vehicle could be the answer to the machine-gun nests on battlefields that in the three months of fighting had cost the Allies almost a million casualties.

Senior officers in the British army, including Lord Kitchener, who inspected the track vehicle, called it a "toy," and scorned it. But Churchill, with keen vision and tireless energy, got behind the idea, and the British navy developed the first tank.

While Churchill was interested in the tank, he also concentrated on problems of the navy. To overcome them and make the fleet even more efficient, he decided to bring back Lord Fisher, almost seventy-four, to his former post as First Sea Lord of the Admiralty. The Devil stood at Churchill's elbow when he made this decision.

Churchill thought that Fisher was a "veritable volcano of knowledge and inspiration." His superb record in the navy started back in the Chinese War of 1859, when he served on H.M.S. *Furious* as a midshipman. A lifetime on warships, rising from midshipman to admiral to First Sea Lord, had given him technical knowledge that was impossible for Winston Churchill to possess. Fisher was supposed to be the greatest seadog since Lord Nelson.

The two men at the top of the navy even looked alike, resembling caricatures of John Bull, although by 1914 "Radical Jack" Fisher had aged. He looked as if he might grow barnacles.

Fisher had sent his friend Churchill notes of advice from Switzerland, signing himself, "Yours till Hell freezes," "Yours to a cinder," "Yours till charcoal sprouts," and so on. Fisher also specialized in gossip and confidential information about naval people, often heading his letters: "PRIVATE! SECRET! BURN THIS!"

Old-timers told stories about Radical Jack Fisher. How, whenever he met a beautiful woman he pursued her until he could dance with her. When ladies came aboard his flagship, he waltzed them to exhaustion on the quarterdeck while the ship's band played his favorite music. He even carried two midshipmen on cruises so they could dance with him. Fisher was married, but as he grew in fame and power he thought his wife beneath his station.

Although Admiral Fisher's great influence on the navy in the past was recognized, many of his contemporaries ridiculed him. He was exceedingly vain, and with the passing of the years he had become erratic. He worried more than in the past, and he was not as daring.

At first the two friends, Churchill and Fisher, got along famously. But with a war on and two men at the Admiralty's helm, both of whom demanded control of details, the pressure on their friendship increased. Radical Jack talked and talked about his pet plan. He would land Russian soldiers on the Baltic coast with the idea of cutting into the heart of Germany. "It will win the war," he said. But when he was asked for particulars, he had nothing to offer.

In late December 1914, a message arrived from Grand Duke Nicholas of Russia that would prove to be fateful. He begged for help: "Could Lord Kitchener arrange for an expedition against the Turks? It would assist our men fighting in that part of the world."

Lord K said that the army could not spare a man. It had more than it could handle in France. Marshal Joffre said that he would resign if even one French soldier was sent to the Dardanelles (the strait between the Aegean and Black seas).

Churchill studied the request and consulted his right-hand man. Fisher gave his answer in a rash of

capitals: "FIRST LORD, I CONSIDER THE AT-
TACK ON TURKEY HOLDS THE FIELD. BUT
ONLY IF IT'S IMMEDIATE! WE CAN SEND A
SQUADRON OF OLD BATTLESHIPS TO FORCE
OUR WAY THROUGH THE DARDANELLES." It
is too bad Fisher did not add: "BURN THIS!"

The idea struck Churchill's fancy. He was delighted
that Admiral Fisher approved. Not only would the
plan ease the pressure on Russia's fighting men, but
food could be shipped to her more easily than by the
northern route. All this would make Russia an even
greater adversary of the Kaiser's armies. And Britain
was already planning to scrap old battleships. They
would be perfect for the plan: obviously ships striking
through the Dardanelles would come under fire from
Turkish shore batteries. But spies had reported them
to be armed with antique cannon. The forts along the
strait could be overcome.

There was some opposition to the plan by Admiral
Sackville Carden, but by January 1915, Winston
Churchill was on fire with the idea. He addressed the
War Council, using eloquence no one present could
match. He supported his startling sentences with details of how the plan would work, details supplied him
by Lord Fisher.

"What about Turkish minefields?" a dissenter asked.
"They're guarded by the shore batteries. And there's a
current in the Dardanelles. If mines are dropped in the
water by the Turks, they'll float downstream. If they
hit a battleship, it will sink."

Churchill had the answer. British trawlers, working

in pairs and protected by destroyers and light cruisers, would sweep the strait free of mines. "The French will send four battleships," he said. And, as a clincher, he added, "We will send the *Queen Elizabeth*. Her powerful sixteen-inch guns will pulverize the shore batteries." This persuaded Kitchener. Although he knew little about the navy, he was impressed by the might of the *Queen Elizabeth*, the most powerful battleship afloat.

The more Churchill talked, with his peerless command of the English language and with his buoyant persuasiveness, the more convincing he became, and more and more Council members joined his idea, even though it ran counter to one of Lord Nelson's maxims, "A warship should never attack a fort."

The Council concluded that the navy could take the Gallipoli Peninsula, which stretched along the east coast of the Dardanelles, and could capture Constantinople. Churchill felt happy, gratified, and sure of success. With his plan succeeding, the war would be a giant step nearer a successful close.

But a month later Lord Fisher dropped a bombshell. He had turned against the plan. Among the first to hear of his revolt was his close friend Admiral John Jellicoe. Fisher wrote him, "I don't agree with a step taken." Then Fisher carried his alarm to Prime Minister Asquith, saying, "The fleet will be severely damaged." The PM, visibly upset, sent for Churchill. The upshot of their conference was that the attack on the Dardanelles would go ahead.

The famous friendship between Churchill and

Fisher cooled. Churchill now found himself in a painful situation. Here he was shepherding one of the war's
most precarious operations, with his chief advisor and
technical advisor firmly against it. Churchill heaped
pressure on the balky First Sea Lord and tried to con-
ciliate him, but it was like talking to concrete.

In spite of arguments behind the scenes, in mid-
March 1915, the allied armada, of sixteen battleships
and a host of smaller vessels, steamed into the narrows
of the Dardanelles. At first the plan ticked like clock-
work. Small, fast warships cut close to shore and attacked the forts, with the trawlers close behind sweeping for mines. At longer ranges, the huge battleships
arched explosive shells into the forts, putting a few of
them out of action. But five ships struck mines and
sank. This unnerved Churchill's representative on the
scene, Admiral John de Robeck. He ordered signal
flags run up that spelled "Withdraw."

It became obvious that to force the Dardanelles and
to capture Constantinople an army would have to be
landed on the Gallipoli Peninsula to work with the
navy. This sounded easy in London, but landing on a
hostile shore is the most difficult of military operations.

In mid-May 1915, the navy off Gallipoli suffered yet
another disaster. The battleship *Goliath* was torpedoed
by a Turkish destroyer and went down, carrying five
hundred and seventy sailors with her. Fisher chose this
dark hour to leave the Admiralty, sending Churchill a
curt note, "I am off for Scotland at once to avoid all
questioning."

In a longer letter, Fisher wrote his former friend in the capitals he loved, "YOU ARE BENT ON FORCING THE DARDANELLES AND NOTHING WILL TURN YOU FROM IT—*NOTHING*. I know you so well." Shortly, he dashed off another to Churchill: "Your tongue is slung amidships and wags at both ends."

In spite of such conduct, and in spite of the barbs Lord Fisher hurled at him, Churchill tried again to persuade the sour admiral to return, but without success. Shortly thereafter, the tragedy at the Dardanelles swamped Churchill; he was forced to resign from his position in the Admiralty that he loved so well.

The calamity at the Dardanelles unfolded like a devilish accordion. Transports carrying allied soldiers to the dreary peninsula had not been loaded correctly, so before they could put infantrymen and artillerymen ashore they had to steam for Alexandria, Egypt, to be reloaded, while Turkish spies walked the docks, taking notes. When the soldiers did land at Gallipoli, German General Liman von Sanders, with the help of eight hundred German officers and sixty thousand hard-fighting Turks, stopped the Allies on the barren cape. Trench warfare began, with drinking water for the invaders hauled all the way from Egypt. Anzacs (the Australian–New Zealand Army Corps) earned fame under drastic conditions because of their courage. After nine months of fighting, Lord Kitchener called the operation off. Casualties for both sides totaled one-quarter of a million men. Gallipoli became one of the saddest defeats in British history.

Lack of success in the campaign would dog Churchill for the rest of his career. Churchill blamed Mr. Asquith for his downfall, overlooking his own part in the tragedy. He could still smile, though. He told friends, "I'm an escaped scapegoat." In spite of the failure, he was offered a small post in the British government, which he declined. Rather than be sidetracked, with a war on, he obtained a lieutenant colonel's commission in the Sixth Royal Scots Fusiliers, a battalion fighting in France.

At first the soldiers disliked Lieutenant Colonel Churchill. He snapped out cavalry commands that they could not understand, and they told each other, "Churchill's all political." But he declared war on lice and made everyone clean up. He took care of the Fusiliers as if they were his own children. His showmanship bubbled up. He painted his French steel helmet blue, so that he would stand out, and occasionally, to show his contempt for German marksmanship, he walked along the top of the trench instead of in it. In the same vein, he had his orderly place a tin bathtub on the top of the trench and empty a few canteens of water in it. Then he peeled off his uniform and took a bath. He loaned his tub to others, making them promise that if the Germans punctured it they would patch up the holes.

Back in London on leave, Churchill plunged headfirst into the political pot, soon proposing that Lord

Fisher be brought back to the Admiralty. This bombshell upset Churchill's friends. The opposition seized
it. Even his wife fretted over his politics. Fisher encouraged him with a weird note that used words like
darts, imploring him to make quick decisions, to shoot
at sight, and not to falter. Backing the eccentric Fisher
cost Churchill political support, but Churchill did not
worry. He did what he thought best.

When he returned to France, he discovered that a
reorganization had left him with a less important job,
so he resigned from the army in May 1916.

The canvas of Churchill's life is so broad that only
part of it can be presented here. In the next few years
he became Secretary of State for War and Air, then
Colonial Secretary, and later Chancellor of the Ex-
chequer.

In 1938, Churchill saw the danger of Hitler and his
Nazis, so he opposed Prime Minister Neville Chamber-
lain's appeasing of the German leader. This in turn led
to Churchill's resigning from the Cabinet. In 1939
Churchill again became First Lord of the Admiralty,
and in 1940, Prime Minister, offering his countrymen
"blood, toil, tears and sweat . . . and victory at all
costs."

During World War II, Churchill, Franklin D. Roosevelt and Stalin led the Allies. Although the British
Empire was not as strong as the United States or the
Soviet Union, Roosevelt and Stalin treated him as an
equal — Churchill's dynamic, pulsing personality saw
to that. At times, especially in America's early days in

the war, Prime Minister Churchill strongly influenced
President Roosevelt. Then, on occasion, he adopted a
puckish manner and referred to himself as "the American President's lieutenant."

In the dark days of World War II, Churchill withstood even greater pressures than in the first great war.
He had seen how the campaigns of the Somme and
Gallipoli had removed young men from the London
streets. Consequently, he preferred operating along
the borders of the Axis countries instead of smashing
into their hearts. This course collided at times with the
views of American military leaders, headed by General
George C. Marshall, who wanted a speedier end of the
Nazi regime so that the Allies could turn their forces
on the Japanese.

In World War II, even at Churchill's advanced age,
his vigor wore out younger assistants. He spouted
memoranda like some kind of fantastic machine.
Under the stresses of his office and as Britain's principal strategist, he grew irritable and hard to work for.
Once, when things were not going right, he yelled at a
staff assistant, "You don't care if we lose the war. You
just want to draw your pay and eat your rations."

Yet in the next hour, Churchill could be humble
and courteous, and show signs of being patient. He
worked to hide his emotions, but on one occasion his
fellows glimpsed the inner Churchill: when he saw
British women standing in long lines to buy food he
burst into tears.

Most Britons and Americans looked up to Churchill

as a moral force, a leader who would bring victory. In his speeches he gripped their imagination when he spouted Churchillian phrases like "Hitler, the bloodthirsty guttersnipe" and "that jackal Mussolini."

The British people astounded most Americans by voting Churchill out of office at the end of the war. It was their way of saying that they wanted no more of the Conservative party, which had blundered in the prewar years, and many blue collar workers believed that Churchill would not help their interests.

But Churchill was not through. In 1946, in Missouri, he made his "Iron Curtain" speech, warning the world of Soviet power and ambition. In 1948 he advocated a federation of free nations in Western Europe, and in 1951 he again led his people as Prime Minister.

In 1953, at the age of seventy-nine, he won the Nobel Prize for Literature. One honor he valued was a proclamation by the American Congress in 1963, signed by President John F. Kennedy, making him an honorary citizen of the United States.

Churchill found time in his long life to write voluminously, chiefly on military history; perhaps his best writing was accomplished in his younger years. He became an accomplished landscape painter. He performed so skillfully with the brush that in 1959 an exhibition of sixty-two of his paintings drew more than one hundred and forty thousand people, and he wrote an instructional book, *Painting as a Pastime*.

Churchill's amazing career as a leader stretched across fifty years. His creed, evidenced as a young man when he left Harrow to take the examinations for Sandhurst three times rather than accept failure, was not to quit. In World War II, with the issue in grave doubt, he preached to his fellow citizens, "Never give in, never give in, *never, never, never, never.* . . . Never yield to force." That was Winston Churchill.

7

PHILIPPE PÉTAIN
"They Shall Not Pass"

GENERAL PÉTAIN stood at attention before the desk of
"Papa" Joffre, his composure and famous self-confi-
dence almost deserting him. Pétain did not know what
to expect from the French commander-in-chief. The
telegram, a bare-bones message, had merely said:
"GENERAL JOFFRE DESIRES TO SEE YOU AT ONCE." What
did this mean? This was February 1916. Papa Joffre
had been shuffling generals like cards.

General Pétain raised his hand in the jerky French
salute as smartly as a young Saint-Cyr cadet and reported.

Joffre smiled and said, "Welcome, Philippe. I need
you." But Pétain still felt wary. He braced himself by
thinking of how he had led a division in the Battle of
the Marne and an army in northern France. He believed that his service had been more than satisfactory.

General Joffre sat behind his desk like a monstrous
bullfrog. His stomach looked as if it were a balloon in
a blue uniform. Scattered across the desk top were a

General Philippe Pétain (left) meeting with General Mondésir at headquarters in the Marne district. (United Press International Photo)

wine glass, plate, knife, fork, spoon, crumbs, pencils, paper, steel helmet, and pistol. He was expressionless. You couldn't read his face; you seldom could.

Joffre motioned Pétain to a straight-backed chair and said, "You look splendid. I'm pleased with your leadership and generalship, Philippe, and now — " In a breath he placed General Pétain on the hottest spot on the globe. The older general motioned to a map tacked against the wall and said, "You will command at Verdun, starting at once. They've been fighting there for four days."

General Joffre paused, as if waiting for the junior officer to speak, but when all he did was to stare at the map Joffre barged on. "You will be resolute. Hold Verdun — no matter what the cost. Realize this, and let this get about — any leader who permits retreat at Verdun will be court-martialed." Then Joffre concluded with an odd sentence: "My friend, now you are easy in your mind." He probably meant that there was no confusion in the blunt directive he had handed Pétain.

The man Joffre was placing in command at Verdun, the fifth child in the Pétain family, was born in 1856 on a farm near Arras, France, that had been in the possession of the Pétains for over a hundred years. Like Joffre, Henri-Philippe Benoni Pétain had received his education from the Jesuits. Schoolwork came easily for Philippe; by nineteen he held a Bachelor of Philosophy degree from a Dominican college. Then something sparked him toward a military career.

After a year's study, he entered Saint-Cyr, the West Point of France. It was a school that at the time stood near the forest of Versailles. Its buildings looked like an inverted quarry, but they hinted at Saint-Cyr's heritage: the five courtyards of the seventy-six-year-old school were named after Napoleon's victories.

Cadet Pétain found life at Saint-Cyr unique. No text books were used, although in the two-year course the cadets studied descriptive geometry, physics, geography, general literature, history, military drill, drawing, and English or German. The library contained only twenty-four thousand volumes, and many of them were rare books, not to be touched except by permission. The library was a sort of sanctuary: only thirty cadets a day — out of three hundred — could enter it. No newspapers were permitted on the grounds, and there were restrictions on cadets talking to each other.

The cadets studied to be either artillerymen, infantrymen, or cavalrymen. (The cavalry was thought to be of greatest importance.) In 1878, Infantryman Philippe Pétain presented himself before the graduation jury. It questioned him closely and passed him.

After leading such a hedged-in life, it is not surprising that many Saint-Cyr graduates of that day bore the mark of its world-apart existence and were considered snobs by their countrymen. This was a time when military officers in every army were regarded almost as a separate race, and many of them looked down their noses at civilians. Large numbers of Saint-Cyrians had resigned from the army, but in 1914 most of them rushed to defend the tricolor. The famous school built love for France into its men, and forty-six hundred graduated cadets fell on World War I battlefields.

Saint-Cyr's rigid life influenced Pétain. He regarded duty as a Holy Grail, but he also mistrusted civilians. It was normal for him to be aloof, and sometimes he could be extremely abrupt. A general under whom he served graded him on report as "Silent, calm, and cold; the enemy of prompt resolution." Another characterized him: "Never talks uselessly." Pétain spent long years on the promotion ladder. Yet when he did gain the recognition that sent him to L'Ecole de Guerre (the School of War) for special study, he received the ordinary, final grade of *Bien* (Good).

Today, Pétain would be called a "late bloomer." It took him thirty-six years to be promoted to colonel and to be known in the army as a sound thinker. By 1914 he had become capable of independent thought. He doubted that artillery could win by itself on a battlefield. To artillerymen this smacked of heresy. Back at the beginning of the century, artillerymen asked, What weapon had been primarily responsible for Napoleon's delivery of an empire to France? Everyone knew the answer: the cannon, of course. Most infantry officers, also in a world of their own, thought that their branch of the army, "the Queen of Battles," was the arm that gained success in battle. The majority of the generals believed that all it took to make victory certain was the sharpshooting infantryman with his bayonet, plus discipline, high morale, and officers imbued to lead forward. Pétain, and a handful of others, thought that other necessary ingredients were firepower and teamwork, and he was not sure that you must always attack.

Two years before the war scourged the peoples of Europe, he commanded the Thirty-third Infantry Regiment. One of its lieutenants was the temperamental, ambitious Saint-Cyr graduate Charles de Gaulle. Each respected the other.

The peacetime days that Pétain spent in the army, and even the two years in the war before General Joffre sent for him, seemed almost insignificant compared to the fiery furnace he found at Verdun. Carrying out Joffre's orders seemed harder than scaling the north wall of the Matterhorn.

While German General Erich von Falkenhayn, leader of the Germans attacking Verdun, could not know Pétain's orders, he could have guessed them. Every German senior leader realized that Verdun and its ring of forts were the pride of France, that Frenchmen loved the ancient city, whose history reached back to A.D. 451, and was sprinkled with famous names — Clovis, King of the Franks; Charlemagne; and Louis XIV. It was a chronicle that also listed two captures of the town by Germans.

General von Falkenhayn concluded that Verdun would be a magnet for Frenchmen, that pride involving the place would cause French soldiers to be rushed there. Falkenhayn's thinking was right: the battle soon

spread over an area of ten square miles, and before it
ended the Germans threw sixty-three divisions against
the Verdun forts — almost a million soldiers — with
France trying to equal that number. Verdun developed quickly into a monster that devoured men.

When word was passed through Verdun's trenches,
concrete pillboxes, and forts that the new commander
was General Pétain, French soldiers smiled. He had
earned a reputation for being careful with men's lives.
They knew, too, that he was a front-line general, a man
of France rather than a man of the Paris boulevards
and nightclubs. But the day after he arrived at Verdun,
the soldiers received a setback. It snowed heavily, and
in the storm they fought in a confused manner that
enabled the Germans to move closer. The mission
Papa Joffre had given Pétain — hold Verdun at all
costs — was tottering. It was a far more intricate thing
to accomplish than it had appeared in Joffre's headquarters.

Pétain attacked his tremendous task by first visiting
the front lines. Then he calmly and methodically reorganized the defenses to make them more efficient,
placing two weeks' rations at key points in case his
defenders were cut off. He realized that supply would
play a big part, and consequently he worked night and
day on the problem. His solution placed pioneer soldiers (field engineers) and territorial troops on the
two railroads leading into the city, with the job of
keeping them in repair. He placed thousands of other
pioneers, also working around the clock in shifts, on

the miserable highway from Bar-le-Duc to Verdun so that the endless chain of trucks could roll to the front with ammunition and other supplies, and so that the wounded could be carried out. The highway became of such vital importance that it became known as the "Sacred Way." Every time a shell plowed into it, or the railroad tracks, pioneers sprang to correct the damage.

On February 26, 1916, Philippe Pétain caught double pneumonia. His aides feared that he was through, but they kept his illness a secret because it would have disheartened front-line fighters. In a little short of a week, he crawled from his bed and struggled into his uniform. He lacked strength, but Papa Joffre stiffened him, saying, "You must hold on to the job!"

Pétain carried out his orders, but he irritated General Joffre by demanding more and more men. Papa Joffre growled like a bear when telegrams arrived at his headquarters signed Pétain, because most of them bore one theme: SEND MORE RESERVES AT ONCE. VERDUN CANNOT HOLD UNLESS I HAVE REINFORCEMENTS. Joffre sent them.

The German side had its troubles. General von Falkenhayn listened to Crown Prince Wilhelm, the Kaiser's son, who said, "Give me fresh soldiers, and I'll advance down both sides of the Meuse River. This will win this battle." It was a gamble, but its chances were good. However, Falkenhayn lost his nerve and told the Crown Prince to attack along the riverbanks on a narrow front. More Germans lost their lives. Then the Germans changed their tactics. They slowed down and

let the French attack. As a result, France began to suffer the heavier casualties.

President Raymond Poincaré visited General Pétain
during the battle. It was an unhappy meeting. Both
men were a bit shy and reserved, and the general
bluntly told the President that France could not expect to win the war under her present government.
Few could be more arrogant than Pétain when he
chose.

With the constant blasting by guns, the earth
around Verdun began to resemble (and still does)
photographs of pockmarked areas on the moon. Nine
French villages were blotted out. The ancient city became a shambles. Still Pétain and his men held on.

People not close to him thought that he had ice
water in his veins instead of blood, but he wrote at the
time about the huge conflict, "My heart contracted
when I saw our young men of twenty going into the
firing line at Verdun with songs and jokes, and I liked
the confident look they gave me as a form of salute.
But what discouragement there was when they returned, whether individually as wounded, or in the
impoverished ranks of their companies!"

By the time the dreadful battle ended in December
1916, eleven months after it began, almost a million
soldiers had become casualties, with France losing almost a hundred thousand more than Germany. Today
a feeling of death still pervades the area. Neither side
won.

Woven into legends about the battle are stories of

Pétain. Frenchmen, especially those living at Verdun, still associate his name with the defense that symbolizes the determination of the French people. During the battle, the word had gone out from Pétain's head-quarters down to the last man: "They shall not pass." Pétain became known as the "Savior of Verdun."

But when political leaders promoted and retired Joffre, Pétain suffered a blow: he was not chosen as commander-in-chief of the French army. President Poincaré wanted almost anyone but the aloof, opinionated and abrupt Pétain. The energetic, charming, vivacious General Robert Nivelle, a subordinate of Pétain's at Verdun, was selected over the heads of several famous generals. If Pétain felt hurt he concealed it. He became a military advisor to the French government, a lonely, backwater job.

The new senior general, Nivelle, fearless on the battlefield, was an odd mixture of politeness and rudeness. He spoke perfect English. This, his assurance, and his alert look had charmed Premier Lloyd George of Britain, who called him the New Messiah and ordered the British generals to cooperate with him.

When the New Messiah took over the wheel of the French army, about the first thing he did was to antagonize many of the British generals, ordering them about as if they were plebes. And at a London dinner party he said, "Confidentially, I am going to organize an offensive so powerful that German machine guns will be overwhelmed. I promise you that I will blast enemy defenses on the stark slopes of the Aisne River and on the heights of the Chemin des Dames." Pétain heard of Nivelle's boasting, but there was nothing he could do.

Nivelle's talk also reached Allied soldiers in the front-line trenches. These men were ready to believe anything that sounded as if the war might end. It would be the fulfillment of their dreams. Nivelle's babbling also passed to spies, and they carried his plan to Germany. Consequently, his mammoth, straight-ahead attacks lacked a prime ingredient: surprise. On the first day, April 16, 1917, approximately 120,000 Allied soldiers suffered death, wounds, or capture. A small mutiny broke out in the French army. There were rumors that others were simmering. Nivelle was through.

Politicians of France, now thoroughly frightened, se-lected Philippe Pétain to be the new commander-in-chief. Pétain, as blunt as an old pickax, told his gen-erals at once that they must be far more cautious in ordering large attacks at German trenches. He saw that machine guns, when placed in defensive strongholds, were ruling the battlefield. He possessed both common sense and boldness enough to break with custom.

Before Nivelle left the army, he and Pétain met in Marie Antoinette's suite in the palace in the forest of Compiègne. They were a contrast in styles. Pétain, fifty-eight, of medium height and sturdy, with a bit of a paunch, wore a ragged, iron-gray mustache that made him look like an old wirehaired terrier. Nivelle was younger, spry and jaunty. He concealed his disappointment by appearing in an immaculate, full-dress blue uniform, his chest ablaze with decorations. Both generals felt uncomfortable. Their conference was as cool as the wine Nivelle served at dinner.

Both avoided talk of mutiny, and they had little to say about the state of the war. The Allied picture looked dismal. German submarines were sinking supply ships at an alarming rate. The scarcity of young men was now showing on London streets more bleakly than after the Gallipoli campaign. French towns were suffering similarly. The United States had entered the war on the side of the Allies, but its national army had to be assembled and trained. That would take a year. The regular United States Army, pitifully small, was spread over forty-eight states, Hawaii, Alaska, and the Philippines; and in 1916–1917 it had failed to overcome the Mexican bandit Pancho Villa.

But as dreary as the war looked to the Allies in 1917, Allied propaganda spread news daily about victories on the Western Front. It seemed remarkable that the front lines had remained in the same general locations for months.

When Pétain assumed the leadership of the French army on May 17, 1917, he was under no illusions. He knew that his position was precarious and that the future of France was in the balance. The morale of his soldiers rested on rock bottom. Some had actively rebelled. The mutineers seemed smarter than some of the generals in Western Europe when they vowed, "We will defend France, but we will not attack machine guns." In some units, the mutineers chanted, "Stop stupidity! We won't go up into the line! Down with the war!" Pétain was confronted with revolt on an unparalleled scale. If it were not stopped, the Germans could annex France.

The mutiny spread. The situation became almost unbearable to loyal French military men. In some regiments there were wholesale desertions. Soldiers got drunk, and their officers lost control. In other units, men said that they would quit unless the food got better immediately. The French press painted the mutiny as even worse than it was and criticized most political and military leaders as inept. Papers with Communistic leanings wrote of the new "freedom" and joy that the Russian Revolution was bringing to Russian soldiers, suggesting that a revolution would help the French army. Some of the French mutineers vowed that they would shoot officers who interfered with them. Discipline seemed a thing of the past. The army and the people of France wanted to stop the ever-lengthening casualty lists that were producing only grief, and to many thousands of soldiers, mutiny appeared the only answer. The rebellion grew until it gripped about half the French army.

In thinking about how to handle the situation, Pétain decided on a strategy of patience and personal contact. He would also order only limited attacks rather than all-out assaults while he waited to see what kind of an army the United States would send to France.

Pétain saw that paperwork was not going to stop the mutiny. He called for his car and drove to the most mutinous units. (He actually visited over one hundred divisions.) He listened not only to officers but to the noncommissioned officers and to any private supposed to be a leader. He talked of the sacrifices that had already been made for France. He ordered an immediate crusade against drunkenness and a more lenient policy for leaves, so that men could visit their homes. Lastly, he adopted Papa Joffre's practice of relieving inefficient leaders: Two generals and forty-one other officers were retired, dismissed, or transferred.

Officers were holding courts-martial to stop the mutineers. Guilty sentences were given to 23,385 and 413 received death sentences. Pétain personally studied the records of the 413 ring leaders and ordered "other punishment" for all but fifty-five, who faced firing squads.

Pétain realized that Nivelle's disastrous offensive was not the sole cause of the mutinies. The French people had resented the "nation-apart" ideas of many senior military leaders for over forty years. Families of men who had been killed since the Battle of the Marne were especially bitter over the slaughter. Pétain preached that his motto was "Victory at the smallest price." He called on the government to control the Communist press for a while and to use influence to see that more favorable stories about the army were printed. By June 1917, Pétain had stopped the mutiny. It was his greatest contribution to his nation's effort in the war.

As the war rolled on, Pétain developed serious limitations, chiefly an inability to work with Allied generals. And at times his pessimism drifted to the ranks, and kept him from taking decisive action in an emergency: he began to believe that no action would succeed. These traits made him unfit to face the great German drives of early 1918. He remained commander-in-chief of the French armies on the Western Front, but was subordinated to the more aggressive Ferdinand Foch, who was promoted to generalissimo of the Allied forces in April of that year.

Sadly enough, the rest of the Pétain story shows him continuing on the downgrade.

In 1925, France turned to him to win a colonial war in North Africa — against the Riffs of mountainous Morocco. This was a war in which French and Spanish politics were uppermost, and France was worried over the possible loss of territory and prestige in the Arab world.

Pétain, now more disdainful and overbearing than ever, rode roughshod over General Louis Lyautey, an able French colonial administrator who had conquered and wisely administered the French zone in Morocco. With age and honors, Pétain was growing increasingly arrogant. But he got the situation in hand, and after fighting for almost a year he declared the war over, saying, "It is a situation for politicians." When he returned to France he found himself out of touch with his countrymen: he was surprised to learn that they had long wanted peace.

In 1934 Pétain served for a short time as Minister

of War. He was accused of being an enemy of France and a friend of Franco, the dictator of Spain.

In 1939 and 1940 Marshal Pétain was in Spain as ambassador when Hitler's armies overwhelmed France early in World War II. France recalled him and made him Premier. Many of his colleagues objected because they foresaw that he would arrange for an armistice with Hitler.

Pétain was eighty-four years old when he became "chief of state" for Nazi-occupied France. It has been written that he was senile, that he bowed to Hitler's wishes and collaborated with the German conquerors. It is hard to say definitely that his mind had eroded, but probably he had become vain enough to believe that by collaborating he alone was enabling France to survive.

When the Allies made the first big amphibious landing in North Africa in late 1942, Pétain ordered French soldiers to resist.

After the war, Marshal Pétain was tried by the French for treason because of his collaboration with the Nazis. He was found guilty, deprived of all honors, and sentenced to death. His old lieutenant, Charles de Gaulle, then President of France, reduced his sentence to life imprisonment in a state prison that was isolated but not without certain comforts. At ninety-five, Pétain died and was buried in the Ile d'Yeu, off the Atlantic coast.

In 1973 his grave was robbed and his seventeen-hundred-pound coffin was stolen by French rightists, who wanted Philippe Pétain interred according to his wish: "At Verdun, with my men." The French government could not overlook his collaboration with the Nazis and, in the same year, returned his body to its grave on the lonely island.

8

BILL BRECKENRIDGE
Lady from Hell

RAIN BEAT DOWN on six hundred Canadians who wore the dark plaid kilt of the Scottish Black Watch. It soaked their greatcoats and packs and splattered against their dish-shaped steel helmets. They slip-slopped past a sign that read: PASSCHENDAELE — 3 MILES. No one said anything.

The Canadians realized that they were heading into one of the bloodiest battles of the war. The titanic struggle at Passchendaele, in Flanders, had been eating up men. It was late October 1917. The battle had been under way for eighty-six days.

Signal Corporal Bill Breckenridge, twenty-three years old, shifted his red-and-white semaphore flags and signal lanterns. Like others in the battalion, he knew that the unit was scheduled to be on call, in reserve, until a general decided that they were needed to influence the struggle. Breckenridge felt confident that somehow he would survive. He wondered how many of the six hundred would be present when the battle was

Bill Breckenridge

over. When would the battle be over? Would it ever end?

Bagpipers of this Forty-second Battalion of the famous Black Watch, Royal Highlanders of Canada, up front just behind the lieutenant colonel, began to skirl, "Happy we've been a'thegither." Heads in the column snapped up. It was music that only the Scots understood, music that had braced their fighters for hundreds of years and had terrorized their enemies. Breckenridge said to one of his signalers, "As long as those pipes skirl, I can go. They send blood flying through my veins."

Bill Breckenridge and his comrades needed all the encouragement possible. They had been hiking toward the fiery furnace in an all-day downpour. Their packs weighed them down, made them sink into mud up to their ankles. They cursed the officers silently for making them carry extra ammunition, extra rations, extra hand grenades, and burdensome entrenching tools. The suck of their boots seemed consonant with the dreary landscape. The grayish-brown fields looked as if they had suffered attacks by earth-eating monsters who had left countless craters, cavities twelve to twenty feet wide by five to fifteen feet deep, which in reality were the work of the mortars and heavy artillery.

An extraordinary deluge shut down the bagpipes. The Canadians marched past a labor battalion that had been filling in craters in the dirt road; the men looked as dulled as the shovels on which they rested. Rain pelting the mud puddles gave the illusion that the chalky-yellow water was leaping to meet the down-pour. The hikers were like ships at sea trapped in the circle of the horizon. The sky, a flattened bowl of dark-gray clouds, except for a light blue streak in the west behind them, heightened the impression that there was no escape. Breckenridge, ordinarily gay, had nothing to say.

The marchers were called by the Germans "Ladies from Hell," a name they applied to soldiers who wore kilts, because of their dress and their fighting qualities. The proud battalions of the Scottish Black Watch could trace their regimental history back to the gentle-men of 1725. It was a history laden with tradition and esprit, on which each member could lean in difficult times.

The hikers plodded around a curve, past stumps of trees standing like forlorn sentinels, past a sign "HELL-FIRE CORNER." A Belgian village had once stood there. Now its ruins testified to the power of artillery. A black-lettered white cloth hung from the least-ruined building: ENJOY TEA & CRUMPETS WITH THE YMCA.

The lieutenant colonel raised his arm, blew a Thunderer whistle, and shouted, "Halt! Twenty-minute siesta." Bill Breckenridge uncoupled his tin mess cup from his belt and skidded toward the sign.

"Boys! Boys!" a voice called from the ruins, "Better stay away from this corner."

"Why?" Breckenridge asked. "Does he shell?"

A YMCA worker in a green uniform with red piping stepped through the ruined doorway. "Does he shell?" he said. "He's got the name and address of this crossroad. When his heavies start throwing high explosives, everything goes up. One shell exploded here killing seventeen and wounding twenty-two. I'll be glad when you leave this joint."

The lieutenant colonel, a pace behind Breckenridge, shouted to the major, "Move the battalion around behind and have 'em queue up on the other side."

In the late afternoon guides reported to the Black Watch battalion to lead it into the trenches about two thousand yards west of Passchendaele. Corporal Breckenridge's squad of signalers paired off for the duty of keeping communication lines functioning.

William Breckenridge had been born in Scotland, and in 1906, when he was twelve, his parents brought him to Canada. They settled in Sherbrooke, Quebec. Eventually there were five boys and one girl in the family. Jim wrote of the family and Bill:

> Dad was superintendent of the Manitoba Steel Foundries, a gay and generous individual, a musician who could play any of the brass instruments. He liked to sing Scottish songs and could reel off Robert Burns by the yard. Our mother, Margaret Pllu, quite religious, was a Salvation Army girl. Dad joined it because of her. I suspect his interest in the Salvation Army was secondary. Mother was our solid rock of strength.
>
> My brother Bill was a bit high-strung and sentimental. He could bawl hell out of you, and in the

next minute have his arm around your neck, telling you to forget it. But Bill made friends easily. He organized school and church theatricals. Loved photography and traveled on school vacations to the West Indies, England, and France to make stills and movies so he could lecture before various groups and clubs.

He was a quick, lithe high school athlete. It was track and field, lacrosse, basketball, skiing, and golf. He also enjoyed hunting squirrels.

Now, Bill had his faults. Liked to play dollar-a-hole on the golf course with carry-overs. You could hear him cursing and swearing if his strokes piled up, but at the nineteenth hole in the clubhouse he would settle down and lead the group in discussions and singing songs.

When the war broke in 1914, we Breckenridges did not think much of Kaiser Bill. We were patriotic and anxious to protect our country, our parents, grandparents, and women folk. It was duty — and there was a chance for adventure. Propaganda played a part. So Bill, my twin Alex, and I — we were eighteen — volunteered. Bill joined the Black Watch, and before he sailed overseas had his picture taken in "Walking-out Dress," kilt and all, down to the dirk in his stocking. He landed in France in the middle of 1915.

A year after the brothers reached France, Jim's regiment was fighting near Hill 70. He became excited when he saw men of the neighboring battalion wearing the kiltie of the Black Watch, in a town into which the Germans had fired thousands of gas shells. It had rained all morning, and because of the damp weather you could see faint clouds of vapor in the streets.

When he entered the forlorn village, in hopes of finding Bill, a captain of the Black Watch wearing a "speaking mask" said in a voice that sounded like a tired foghorn, "Soldier, the undertaker is going to write 'Died of mustard gas' on your death ticket unless you snap on your mask — quick."

Jim inquired along the streets for his brother as best he could, mumbling through a mask not designed for communication. Finally, he saw a telephone pole that was lashed to a foundation of a house by a maze of wires. He pushed aside a gasproof curtain, removed his mask as he entered the cellar, and shouted, "Has anyone seen Bill Breckenridge?"

Bill hugged him and burst into tears. In a moment, he regained his composure and said, "Major, shake hands with Jim. My kid brother."

The two brothers moved into a room that held the remnants of a furnace. A goat walked around a pile of coal. "The real boss here," Bill said. "Big Goat's our mascot. He even ate a cartridge belt. Loves that damned orange marmalade and bully beef. I've had enough of 'em to last me till kingdom come." With Big Goat as a witness, the brothers exchanged family news and experiences. For both, their meeting near Hill 70, before the Canadian Highlanders entered Passchendaele, was a never-to-be-forgotten moment.

At Passchendaele, the Forty-second Black Watch participated in the Third Battle of Ypres — "Wipers," the soldiers called it. It was a series of desperate, headlong attacks by soldiers of the King against equally determined soldiers of the Kaiser, near the village. (The town's name had been given to the whole, ill-starred offensive, planned and ordered by British General Sir Douglas Haig.)

General Haig was becoming controversial. But he was not a glory seeker. At the beginning of the year he had written to his friend Lord Derby, "If Premier Lloyd George has a man in his eye who will run this great Army better than I am doing, let him appoint him without more ado. You will find that I am sufficient of a patriot to withdraw as a man, and I trust gracefully."

However, Haig, experienced leader of unimpeachable character, could be as changeable and as stubborn as the weather in his native Scotland. In 1916 he had refused to give way to Papa Joffre's request to attack in the Somme River country because he believed that it would cost too many lives, but now in Flanders he gave in to Pétain, who was begging him to keep the German armies occupied while he nursed the French armies after the mutinies.

If General Haig had searched from the English Channel to Switzerland he could not have found a worse place to stage his attacks. He had been warned by the Belgians that heavy bombardment would wreck the complex drainage system in the reclaimed Flemish lands, but he went ahead. During August, the wettest in history, countless streams in the chalky Passchendaele country had overflowed their banks, and the water was trapped. Few roads existed, and to make some of them passable engineers laid hundreds of thousands of planks. Haig wrote to Premier Lloyd George of the drenched country: "The valleys are choked with water. They are transformed into long stretches of bog, impassable except for a few well-defined tracks, which became marks for the enemy's artillery. To leave these tracks risks death by drowning." Haig's selection of the Passchendaele area for his huge offensive, an area in which the Germans sat on the high ground, was an inexcusable error.

On the first day of the straight-ahead offensive, General Haig had lost sixty thousand men. This sacrifice yielded but three or four miles of swamp. In the entire Passchendaele campaign he would lose men at the rate of four thousand a day.

Corporal Bill Breckenridge wrote of his entry into the miserable, swampy area: "The Boche were shelling us as we left the muddy road near Passchendaele village at a sign marked 'California Trench.' My heart was almost jumping out of place, and I felt weak in the stomach. The British Tommies had done their share. The Australians were also in it; and the French were on the flank. Now it was up to us Canadians. I felt better in California Trench than on the road coming in, but the trench was flooded with two feet of water."

The Canadian Scots worked to bail out dugouts and

to drain the trench. In the flat terrain, there seemed to be no low spot for the water to flow.

William Breckenridge continued his written description, "A flotilla of German bombers sailed majestically over us without opposition. 'Whoof-Crump! Sizz-Plunk! Plunk!' went the bombs. We rushed to get clear of the planes, but there was no place to hide."

The task of bailing out was almost finished when German shells of the naval type started falling. These shells traveled at a rate of more than a mile per second. When they sprayed iron over the marshy landscape, Bill Breckenridge and his half-dozen signalers crawled into a soupy dugout.

Breckenridge decribed his feelings as his battalion settled down to protect its trenches and to be on call as a reserve: "There was not a safe place anywhere. Yet the lads tried to be happy and to help one another. When a soldier goes into the trenches, he worries over whether he will get hit or not. But at Passchendaele it was different. Each and every man began to feel that he was in a sure deathtrap."

Bill Breckenridge illustrated his thoughts about the wounded by telling of his friend Porky: "When German shells thundered down, Porky cried, 'I'm hit! I'm hit! They got me in the left armpit.' Then Porky dashed for a corrugated-iron shack ten yards away, as if it could shelter him against the cannonade.

"I ran to an artillery sergeant and asked for a knife so I could rip Porky's sleeve away. When I got back the shrapnel was humming and whining, as it came down

130 BOLD LEADERS OF WORLD WAR I

from every possible angle. Stretcher bearers were staggering through the mud with men who had been hit. I found Porky at the dressing station. His wound was not serious. He had a different expression on his face. He was in the best of spirits. His sadness over being hit was really gladness. He knew he was leaving Passchendaele."

One of the serious problems the Canadians were up against was the difficulty of obtaining drinking water. The weather turned hot. The men found that they could stand the stench of the battlefield, but they suffered from thirst. Stagnant water in the trenches and shell holes tortured them. A water famine stared them in the face. Each man had been issued two canteens of water — water that had to last for twenty-four hours and serve for washing, shaving, and bathing. At night, details of men, laden with canteens, had to find their way to the rear to bring back drinking water.

The nights were more horrible than the days, with red and yellow flashes from around-the-clock artillery, and flares reflected in the low-hanging night clouds. The crash of the shells seemed louder after dark. Near the Canadians were batteries of trench mortars that barked without stopping. Sleep — in the mud under such conditions — was almost impossible.

On the beautiful moonlit night of October 30, 1917, attack orders came, and Corporal Breckenridge's battalion crawled over the top of the trench into No-Man's-Land and walked toward the Germans. Four enemy observation balloons above Passchendaele

Ridge looked like weird posters in the blue-black sky. It was cold and windy. Bill's signal lamp banged into his shoulder. Occasionally a burst of machine-gun bullets whip-cracked over the men. Flares from the German trenches arched above them. The men lay in mud, and no one moved until the ghastly lights flickered out. Then the Canadians jumped up and tore from shell hole to shell hole, ever closer to the enemy.

Finally, in the lovely moonlight, the Germans saw the attackers, and sent sheets of flame and bullets. Bill Breckenridge wrote, "My memory flickered back to my squirrel-hunting days. To think of the fear that must have filled them when they knew they were being hunted to death. Now I felt like a squirrel."

After hand-to-hand fighting, the Canadians captured a German trench and sent prisoners to the rear. It seemed to Bill Breckenridge that he had always been at Passchendaele with its mud and death. Now, looking at the disorganized German prisoners, he thought there was hope of the battle ending; they appeared woebegone and forlorn.

But early in November the Germans came back in waves, right at the Black Watch. When the blow struck, Breckenridge's battalion commander shouted, "Signals! Flash this message back to headquarters about this counterattack."

Bill's friend Spud took the assignment. He clambered to the top of a captured concrete pillbox that had housed machine guns. Spud fumbled with his signal lamp. "I can't get the message through," he yelled at Bill. "Will you try?"

Breckenridge climbed the ladder. He shivered and trembled with excitement as machine-gun bullets bit into the concrete. A shell burst overhead, spraying the pillbox and the muddy ground with a hail of three-quarter-inch iron balls. Bill could not understand why he was not hit.

Breckenridge flashed a recognition signal, then called headquarters with a dash-dot-space-dot-space — and four dots. But headquarters did not reply. He sent the coded message again: "Germans counterattacking. Take counterattack action." Just as he completed the last *n*, Bill glimpsed a sudden burst of light acknowledging his signal. "Stay up there, please," the lieutenant colonel called, "and send two more."

After that crisis was resolved, three German stretcher bearers approached the pillbox under a Red Cross flag. They appeared to be carrying a member of the Black Watch. It was a tense moment. Could this be a German trick? The lieutenant colonel halted the Germans, drew his pistol, and ordered the signalers to cover him. Then he walked forward to investigate. In a moment he waved the Germans through with their pitiful burden.

Because of the bravery and devotion of thousands of Allied soldiers, particularly Canadians like William Breckenridge, Passchendaele village was captured on November 6, 1917, and the bitter hundred-day battle came to an end.

William Breckenridge survived fighting at Amiens, Cambrai, and a two-week leave in England. Just before the Armistice in 1918 he was promoted to sergeant. His brother Jim wrote:

*After the Armistice, when Bill, Alex, and I re-
turned to Canada, times were as hard as flint. To
get started again in civilian life, we were each paid
a bonus of $420 for over four years' service. We
soon found ourselves doing menial chores, such as
cutting grass, at ten to fifteen cents an hour. Bill
landed a job in Manitoba in Dad's company as
nightwatchman and fireman.*

*There was intense criticism of political and
military leadership that had brought such terrible
waste of life and time. Bill became outspoken, but
he remained an optimist. He helped young people by organizing and coaching lacrosse and junior
hockey teams.*

Later, Jim gave Bill a job in his paint manufactur-ing company in Montreal, the start he needed. Bill became general manager in charge of finances and sales. He married Lorna Davis in 1937. They were de-voted, but had no children. He followed a hobby, be-coming director of the Summerlea Golf Club of Mon-treal and enjoyed good times there with his friends. Bill Breckenridge died in 1959, almost a year after the death of his wife.

Jim Breckenridge wrote: "A word I did not tell

about Brother Bill and those dreadful days at Passchendaele. He said he was wallowing in the muck, and that he looked down at his kilt. He had cleaned the plaid as best he could. He thought of the traditions of the Black Watch. Tears came to his eyes. He said it was the old story: 'Highlanders die but never surrender.' "

9

CARL MANNERHEIM
The Knight

NINETEEN-YEAR-OLD CADET MANNERHEIM tugged the sheets and blankets around the head of the dummy, smoothed out his bed, and skidded downstairs and out of the School for Cadets at Hamnia, Finland. He was tired of being confined to his barrack room for weeks on end for trivial offenses, and he was in the mood for entertainment. He believed that the dummy would fool the inspecting officer.

Forty-eight hours later, ex-Cadet Mannerheim stood on the street — expelled. He felt furious and frustrated. He had not been given a chance to tell his side of the situation, nor had he received a paper or certificate to show that he had attended the academy for four years.

Actually, this prank of 1886 was one in a long list of battles between Mannerheim and the school authorities. The school finally won the campaign. He was out.

One crisis after another confronted Carl Mannerheim throughout his turbulent life, but this one was of special import.

Young Mannerheim liked to boast. He told his fellow cadets, before he departed, "I'm going to the Russian cavalry school. I'll have no trouble. The next time you see me I'll be wearing the uniform of an officer in the Czar's army." His comrades howled with laughter. They liked Mannherheim and understood his tendency to brag. They told one another, "At times Carl's head is too big for his hat."

Ex-Cadet Mannerheim could not obtain a transcript, but he had studied Russian in the cadet school and felt confident that with more study he could earn a high school diploma in Russia. This would get him into the Nikolaevski Cavalry School. Mannerheim was extremely self-confident, obstinate, and ambitious. He was also anxious to prove himself to his cadet friends and to the new and popular superintendent of the Hamnia school, General Carl Enckell.

Mannerheim lacked money for food or for hiring a tutor, but he obtained it from relatives and studied Russian in St. Petersburg (now Leningrad) under a Cossack captain. It was a setback to Mannerheim when he discovered that the Russian language under the captain seemed different from the one he had wrestled with in Finland. However, after a year's devotion to books, Mannerheim gained admittance to the Russian cavalry school.

Although he was a foreigner, Mannerheim graduated (in 1899) near the top of his class. But he was disappointed with his first station, a lonely post near the German frontier. There was no threat of war to

Field Marshal Carl Mannerheim in his dress uniform. (United Press International Photo)

keep the officers alert in the Russian dragoon regiment. Had it not been for the interesting problems of training horses and recruits, Carl Mannerheim might have resigned.

But life changed. In a year he was transferred to the famous Chevalier Guards and selected for duty in the huge Winter Palace of Czar Alexander III in St. Petersburg. Strikingly handsome, young Lieutenant Mannerheim enjoyed wearing the Guards' uniform: white blouse with silver-laced collar and cuffs, tight-fitting white buckskin breeches, black patent-leather jackboots that cradled his kneecaps, and a shiny helmet surmounted by a silver two-headed Russian eagle six inches high. Sometimes he carried a heavy cavalry saber, at others a rapier-like sword. His bearing, better-than-average height, and classic profile earned him nicknames: "The Knight" and "The Last of the Vikings." He was one of the handsomest men in St. Petersburg.

Life around the Czar was a world apart from the existence of the masses of Russians, but being near the ruler entranced Mannerheim. He wrote in his *Memoirs*, "This duty gave me the feeling of coming into close contact with Russian history." It also helped, in 1892, to gain him a wife, Anastasie Arapov, daughter of a deceased Russian general, who had powerful connections.

It was not a happy marriage, although they had two daughters. He was Lutheran, she Orthodox. He was full of energy and thought her indolent. He liked riding, hunting, and outdoor trips. She liked the court, society, and entertaining. She thought his egotism hard to bear, and when he occasionally lapsed into sarcasm, she thought him impossible. The Mannerheims discovered that they had to live chiefly on her money because the pay of a Russian lieutenant was meager, and he needed to buy uniforms, boots, shotguns, hunting rifles, saddles and other equipment for horses, polo ponies, and horses for show and in the field.

The family's troubles drifted into the Winter Palace as gossip. This caused Mannerheim worry, but it did not hinder his standing in the army or with the Czar. When that strong monarch died in 1894, Mannerheim was thrilled to be selected as one of the bodyguards for the coronation of Nicholas II and was proud because his post was close to the throne.

Mannerheim became well known in St. Petersburg. He was valuable because the Czar had over a thousand horses in his stables and no one knew more about them than "The Knight." But he was not popular with everyone. Some Russians disliked him automatically because he came from a family, originally Swedish, whose members had been Finnish patriots for over a century.

Ill-feeling existed between the Finns and the Russians. Finland had been part of Russia since 1809 and had been allowed considerable self-government. This was a source of trouble because the Finns had more rights than the Russians, and they resented Russian efforts to take away their freedom. Mannerheim made no bones about his loyalty to Finland. At times, he would say, "Remember, I'm a Finn." This was like rubbing sandpaper on the back of a Russian's neck.

And some Russian officers criticized Mannerheim for being "too professional." Indeed, he thirsted inordinately for recognition. He wanted to show his friends back in the Finnish cadet school that it had been a great mistake to discharge him, and he wanted to be known as a superior officer. But about 1902, his personal life, so important to his official life, received a jolt: his wife left him and took their two daughters to France. She never returned.

Mannerheim nonetheless saw his chance to gain a rung on the promotion ladder. In 1904, Japan had begun a war by a surprise attack on the Russian fleet cooped up in Port Arthur on Korea Bay. Mannerheim readied his equipment. General Aleksei Brusilov, who would become famous himself in World War I, advised Mannerheim, then a lieutenant colonel, "Don't go to this insignificant and unpopular fight. Save yourself for a world war." But Mannerheim was off to the Far East as an executive in a cavalry regiment. (In his restless, adventure-packed life, he would serve in five wars.)

When he arrived at the front he was shocked to find soldiers often drunk, horses neglected, and an unready regiment. All the while, this unit had a mission of helping to defend the five hundred miles of railway line from Port Arthur north to Harbin, Manchuria.

Mannerheim convinced his colonel that he could improve the regiment. He organized a system of mounted patrols to scout the Japanese lines, and on his favorite horse, Talisman, he led some of the patrols himself, and in such daring fashion that some of his brother officers asked each other, "What's the matter with Lieutenant Colonel Mannerheim? He rides as if he were seeking a bullet." On one reconnaissance, Captain Prince Eldarov, riding at his side, fell mortally wounded. On another, Mannerheim's horse was shot.

Mannerheim suffered from rheumatism, but it did not keep him at the end of the war from leading cavalry on a daring raid behind Japanese lines. He won three decorations and proved to himself, and to the Russian cavalry, that he was a fearless front-line leader who possessed remarkable ability to keep his head and courage in crises. When the fight went against his regiment, it was Mannerheim who became its rallying point. Bravery on the battlefield won him not only medals but promotion to colonel.

By the time the war ended in 1905, a Russian defeat, Mannerheim had concluded that the Russian soldier was easily led and easily tempted, but when treated fairly by competent leaders he would fight to the end no matter how great the odds. However, Mannerheim observed that there was an undersupply of capable senior officers and that the vacillation of the Czar had helped to lose the war.

Soon after the Japanese sent the Russian fleet to the bottom in 1905, serious trouble flared at the Winter Palace, where soldiers fired into a crowd of protesters. The lid flew off the political situation. It was easy for

revolutionists to gain support; the war had been unpopular and there were social tensions that threatened
to rip Russia apart.

Because of a general strike and because numbers of
railroad stations had been set on fire, it took Carl
Mannerheim thirty-one days to cross Siberia and Russia on the transcontinental railroad to St. Petersburg.
He saw workers, drunk with excitement, disarming
police and soldiers, and mobs hunting Jews as scape-
goats. Russia was paralyzed until Nicholas II issued a
manifesto giving the people more liberty — concessions
he withdrew as soon as he could. Mannerheim was
being educated in how a violent revolution can cost
lives and wreck property, and also in how a czar could
change his mind.

After his most unusual train trip, Mannerheim, on
leave in Helsinki, Finland, came under the eye of the
Russian secret police because they knew that, although
he was a top-flight Russian army officer, he was a Finnish patriot first. In Helsinki he saw the effects of the
"Russification" of his country, and he felt despondent
because Nicholas was now withdrawing the privileges
that he had promised the Finns they could keep.

Suddenly a wire arrived "requesting" that Colonel
Mannerheim report at once back in St. Petersburg to
the Czar's chief of staff. This led to one of the strangest
requests ever received by an army officer in any
army.

General Palitsyn, an old man past retirement age,
received Mannerheim in the St. Petersburg headquar-

ters with correctness. He began by talking as if he were inquiring about the ponies Mannerheim might ride in next Sunday's polo match.

"You look well, Mannerheim. You're always fit. How do you do it? You're in fine shape, aren't you? How was Helsinki? The records show you as thirty-nine. I can hardly recall being so young. Now here's a secret mission approved by the Czar. You have been selected to ride through Asia, about eighty-five hundred miles. We estimate it will take two years in the saddle. Do you feel up to it? Do you want to go? Let me talk; you may answer later."

Colonel Mannerheim fought to retain his calm.

Palitsyn rattled on, "You'll find few maps." His eyes twinkled. "Just rumors and erroneous directions."

Palitsyn handed Mannerheim a line sketch. "Colonel, if you accept this assignment, you'd cross the Caspian Sea to Krasnavodsk, then go a thousand miles by train to Samarkand and by stagecoach to Osh. Then it will be saddles and pack horses across part of the magnificent 'Roof of the World' to Kashgar, through eastern Turkestan to Ak-su. You'll wind through the snowy peaks and deep valleys of the Tien Shan Mountains, touch Mongolia, and follow caravan paths across the Gobi Desert. Then into China proper, entering the huge gate at the western end of the Great Wall. You'll be eating sand again as you skirt the Wall to Liangchow, and on to Lanchow. You'll be tested by hundreds of miles of mountainous, bandit country to Utaishan, to call on the Dalai Lama, ruler of Tibet.

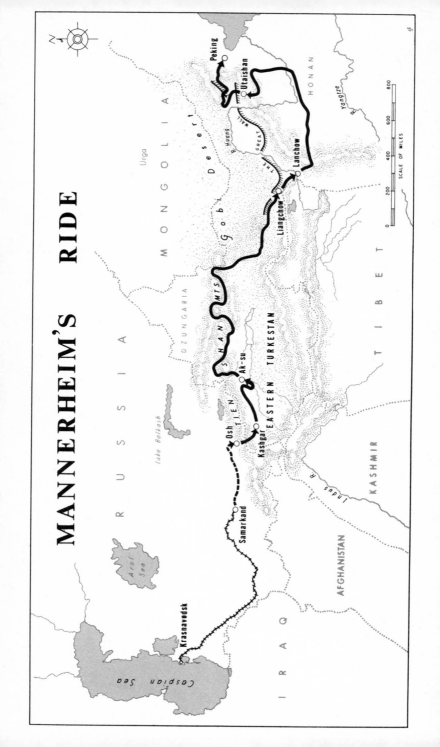

MANNERHEIM'S RIDE

Now to the finish — a long, hard jaunt to Peking. Have a seat, Mannerheim."

General Palitsyn opened a folder marked SECRET and cleared his throat. He slipped unconsciously into an abrupt tone, one he had used in his long service to give orders. "Colonel, memorize your mission and route — no telltale papers. Carry Finnish papers, in case you are stopped. We'll list you as a Finnish scientist. All letters you receive and write — arrange this — must have no mention of Russia. Under no circumstances will you reveal that you are an officer of the Czar. Gather information on Asia and China. There will be some mapping for you to do. Details later. Your recommendations for defensive positions are desired. We want facts about that oasis at Ak-su. We want to know how well defended Lanchow is. You can see that in case of war with China your information will be invaluable to Russia."

Mannerheim glued his eyes to the sketch. Two years in the saddle! Eighty-five hundred miles! If he went, would he ever come back?

"We are calling this an archaeological expedition," the general said. "Dr. Paul Pelliot of France will be along. You'll meet him at Tashkent.

"What about him?" Mannerheim asked. "Who would be in command? He or I?"

"Don't give the professor a thought. He's going only as part of a cover plan to throw off Chinese suspicion. You'll have complete independence. There's no trouble at all with the professor."

Mannerheim fought with himself over the decision. He was most anxious to be promoted, but the secret mission appeared to block him no matter how he decided. A two years' absence would take away opportunities to scale the promotion ladder. If he declined, he would not advance because of the displeasure his refusal would roil up in General Palitsyn and the Czar. With Mannherheim's wife and children gone, life in Russia would not be homelike. On the trip, he would experience severe hardships, but it would be life in the outdoors, an unparalleled adventure among strange peoples. *If* he survived, he would gain distinction and fame.

In the Japanese war Mannerheim had discovered that he liked exploring uncharted land. He studied secret files in Palitsyn's office about part of the area he would cover. The more he concentrated on the trip the more enthusiastic he became. It looked like a one-in-a-thousand adventure.

Finally, Mannerheim accepted and began preparing himself by reading of Marco Polo's travels in the thirteenth century, as well as everything else he could find on Asia. He took crash courses in archaeology, anthropology, and photography — including the developing of films. He interviewed people who had traveled in parts of Asia, but they could tell him little. Many problems would have to be solved on the trail.

Mannerheim told his friends good-bye in St. Petersburg on July 6, 1906.

In Samarkand, two Ural Cossacks reported to him to

serve as helpers on the expedition. The Czar himself
had wired the local commander to select two out of
forty Cossacks who had volunteered. These were hardy
peasant soldiers, born on horseback, whose forebears
had not been serfs for centuries. In his *Memoirs,* Mannerheim described the two Cossacks as "fine lads." He
believed that they would stay the course.

When "Mr." Mannerheim arrived at the old city of
Tashkent and met Dr. Pelliot, his troubles started.
Mannerheim opened the conversation by talking of
the Mongolian inhabitants and the Moslem religion,
but when he got down to brass tacks, Pelliot, cranky
and impatient, exploded. He learned for the first time
that his three Cossacks and the two with Mannerheim
would obey Mannerheim rather than himself. And
Pelliot became even more furious when he discovered
that Mannerheim had not brought the ten thousand
francs promised by the Russian high command for expenses.

When the two leaders discussed routes, the scientist
snapped, "Listen! You may come with me but *not* as a
member of my expedition. I will not be responsible for
any difficulties with you, and I will decide exactly
where you may travel."

While Mannerheim struggled to hold his temper
and tried to think how to deal with such a difficult
personality, Pelliot solved the situation by disclosing to
the expedition's physician Mannerheim's real occupation and his secret mission. Mannerheim was not the
type to excuse such a breach of security. Consequently,

he parted from the scientist and rode on with his two Cossacks, Lukanin and Rachimjanov, an interpreter (who was barely proficient in the languages they would encounter), a servant or two, and pack animals. This was the last Mannerheim saw of Dr. Pelliot.

Before the two parted, to proceed by separate routes, Dr. Pelliot promised to meet Mannerheim somewhere on the trip. They did keep in touch by letters, but Pelliot changed his plans and no rendezvous occurred.

Mannerheim's trip was an epic of its kind. He kept a meticulous diary in cloth-covered notebooks. Although he thought his account dull, it tells of trouble on the trails, of breathtaking scenery, of curling up in sheepskins to spend the night in snowdrifts, of riding on icy paths in the Tien Shan Mountains, where the winds howled so fiercely there was danger of the horses being blown into the valley below. He described his scientific observations, hunting for food in all kinds of weather, bouts with rheumatism. The Cossack helper Rachimjanov became ill — probably from pneumonia — and had to be sent back by a mail convoy. Mannerheim described exhausted horses, and peoples and customs stranger than any he had envisioned. He wrote of the happiness he felt when his party left wild country to ride through the fields and streets of a village. He became tired of sleeping on the ground in freezing tents. When he could, he spent the night in peasants' huts. By error he slept one night in the bed of a leper. At one point he became ill from sunstroke.

His luck turned when he acquired a cook, Chang,

who made campfire meals a joy. But still the party underwent ordeals: the filth of Central Asia and the blast-furnace heat of the Gobi Desert.

Mannerheim guided his tiny unit safely through mountainous bandit country to the temporary quarters of the Dalai Lama, although monks stoned the party en route. Mannerheim worried because he lacked an appropriate present for the religious leader. He gave him two shiny pistols and apologized. Fortunately, the Dalai Lama thought this amusing.

Finally, on July 25, 1908, Mannerheim completed the last leg of his journey by train, arriving in Peking and reporting with pride to Colonel Korilov, the Russian military attaché, that his mission was complete. Then Mannerheim had the task of saying good-bye to the two men he liked best on his fantastic trip: the Cossack Lukanin and the cook, Chang. Mannerheim, although lean and tough as a steel spike, felt tired. He vacationed for two weeks in Japan, then returned to St. Petersburg and reported to General Palitsyn.

"Congratulations," the general said. "The Czar wants to hear your report from you personally. When he's ready, he'll send for you. Twenty minutes' talk by you should be sufficient."

When Colonel Mannerheim stood before the little man with the trim brown beard and flowing mustache, who wore a white military blouse and drab breeches thrust into polished boots, he was facing one of the most powerful autocrats on earth. So vast was the power of Czar Nicholas II that he could, if he chose, arrest his subjects and pass sentence on them. Unfortunately, he was a weak character of limited intelligence, scantily educated. Consequently, he did not comprehend the lives and aspirations of his subjects, particularly the workers and land-hungry serfs, nor did he choose officials who would help him to rule firmly but justly. Still, he was the Czar, protected in 1908 by a shield of majesty. Subjects summoned before him fought to prevent their knees from knocking. But not Mannerheim. While he was most eager to please the ruler of Russia, he never forgot that he was not a Russian subject but a Finn.

The Czar thought himself a soldier, but he depended upon personal favorites to advise him on the problems of commanding the armed forces. His trusted friend Palitsyn had recommended that he listen to Mannerheim, so Nicholas stood, according to custom, while Mannerheim talked of his ride through Asia for one hour and twenty minutes.

When Mannerheim apologized for talking so long, the Czar smiled, thanked him, and said, "What are your plans?"

Mannerheim, never one to skip an opportunity, replied quickly that he had missed promotion during his trip and that he wanted to command a regiment.

"Don't worry about missing promotions," the Czar said. "Few in history have been privileged to make such a ride. I'm glad that Russia has your records."

(When Mannerheim was seventy and back in Finland, he presented his valuable diaries to the Finno-

Ugrian Society. He apologized for the roughness of the writing, explaining that most of it had been accomplished under difficult conditions and that he had lacked time to smooth it out. In his report, and in his *Memoirs*, he repaid Dr. Pelliot for his overbearing rudeness by not mentioning him.)

By the time Russia plunged into World War I, Mannerheim was forty-seven years old, an experienced officer who commanded two regiments of the Czar's cavalry in Poland. Although he relished his job, he found it too far from his beloved Finland, and he disliked the Russians' corrupt policies and their oppression of the Poles. But Mannerheim had climbed the promotion ladder. The Czar had elevated him to *général à la suite* (personal aide), an honored post that let him wear the Czar's monogram on his epaulettes, placed him in Imperial General Headquarters, and gained him entrance to the Czar's offices and quarters. He and Nicholas became friends and enjoyed hunting together.

Mannerheim liked the little man personally, but he could not fail to see that he was a weak ruler and insipid. At Imperial Headquarters, Mannerheim was appalled by the inefficiency. The supply system was rickety, great numbers of poorly trained units would have to be employed in a war, and there was no emphasis on leadership. To overwhelm her enemies, Russia would have to depend upon mass attacks, featuring wave after wave after wave of infantrymen sweeping forward—to become fodder for enemy cannon.

World War I surprised the Russian people. In towns scattered over the vast country, the first the great majority knew of the worsening European situation was when telegrams arrived from the Czar ordering all men between the ages of eighteen and forty-three to report to the colors. In Cossack towns on the Mongolian frontier the men generated enthusiasm, while the women watched in admiration and doubt. Horsemen carrying red flags galloped up and down the streets shouting, "War! War! War!"

But no one knew who the enemy was — the telegram did not say. "Can it be the Japanese again?" people asked one another. Some said, "Of course not. *England!*" Wise men ventured, "Turkey!" Then another telegram placed the blame squarely on the Kaiser. The story went that so great was the feeling for war it was difficult to eat in a Moscow restaurant because you had to stand while people took turns raising their glasses "To Holy Russia!" "To our glorious leader, the Little Father!" and so on.

The war was hardly a month old when Mannerheim won the coveted decoration of the Cross of St. George for bravery against the Austrians, in the same campaign in which Fritz Kreisler fought.

When the tide turned in November 1914, and the Russians reeled back in full retreat, General Mannerheim stood out because of his character and intellect. His divisions became obstacles to the Germans, delaying them and making them pay for every mile of ground.

Combat brings out the best and the worst in men. Mannerheim could be tender. General Sir Alfred Knox, the British military attaché, described a scene after a battle when a Russian mother came forward to find her dead son, one of Mannerheim's men. Mannerheim kissed the dead Lancer and said, "I only wish I were in this boy's place."

When the Germans swept deeper into Russia, Mannerheim saw the terrible "lacks" in the Czar's armies: lack of artillery and artillery ammunition; lack of rifles for infantrymen, who had been brought to the front to fight without weapons and who had been told they were to arm themselves when other men fell; and lack of food.

In early September 1915, with his armies staggering ever backward, the Czar bowed to the influence of his wife. (She was more forceful than he but even less competent. And she was under the evil spell of Gregory Rasputin, one of the most sinister men in history.) Consequently, the Czar removed the rigid disciplinarian Grand Duke Nicholas as commander-in-chief of the Russian armies and took his place. Mannerheim felt that this was a blow to Russia; as much as he liked the Czar personally, he knew that he was unqualified for such a command.

By late 1916 morale was crumbling faster. Back of the fighting lines soldiers were selling their equipment. Bread riots broke out in St. Petersburg. Starvation and misery cast shadows on the cities. By early 1917, red banners of revolution were appearing everywhere. Had it not been for the uncomplaining, hardworking women of Russia, revolution would have arrived sooner.

A network of committees fastened themselves on Russian army units. The soldier-members voted the best course of action. On some parts of the long battle lines, infantrymen cut telephone lines to the artillery so that no attack could be made. Mannerheim stood out in the confusion: his units retained their discipline. But later he wrote sadly, "The high command did nothing to stem the revolutionary tide."

On March 16, 1917, Czar Nicholas II abdicated in favor of his brother, Grand Duke Michael. Mannerheim said, "This was a ray of hope, but Michael abdicated, too." Anarchy spread. The Executive Committee of the Workers' and Soldiers' Deputies Council, called Soviet for short, tried to run the war. When soldiers were no longer required to salute their officers, all semblance of discipline vanished. Most soldiers now dressed in as slovenly a manner as peasants.

The situation became topsy-turvy. Robberies increased. Railroad stations were blown up. The navy mutinied. The peasants revolted, adopting the slogan "We want peace and land." The provisional government, which had taken over from the Czar, could not deal with affairs and became paralyzed. A small but fanatical group of radicals, the Bolsheviks, were growing increasingly powerful. In the worst military units, soldiers were killing their officers.

Mannerheim decided that his thirty years' service to Russia, duty under two Czars, had ended. He was in Odessa at the time, recuperating from a foot injury he had received when his horse fell with him. A telegram arrived from General Dukhonin, commander-in-chief at army headquarters, depriving him of his command, but hinting that he might continue to serve if he made a formal request to do so; the men in power were suspicious of Mannerheim's connections with the Czar.

Mannerheim answered by letter, saying that he had already given up his command. He decided secretly to leave the Black Sea resort and return to Finland. This would call for a journey through what was rapidly becoming "enemy country" for officers. How was he to get through a thousand-mile gauntlet of mutinous soldiers?

For the dangerous trip, he boldly decided to wear his best uniform, with its hated epaulettes. "I would be uneasy wearing a disguise," he told an aide.

He then obtained the use of a private railroad car and had it hooked onto a train that could be expected to roll into St. Petersburg in two days. But there were delays and uncertainty. Along the Dnieper River the train crawled around a bog and stopped at a station. On the platform was a pool of blood. The conductor confided in Mannerheim, "Soldiers just shot General Dukhonin." Mannerheim did not disclose his feelings, but it was a bad time to be one of the Czar's generals.

The trip to St. Petersburg took six days. Here Mannerheim found difficulty in leaving Russia. He could not obtain the necessary permit. Finally, he was given a paper saying that he was a Finnish citizen. This saw him through; he arrived in Helsinki, Finland, in mid-December of 1917.

An event took place in Helsinki that meant more to Mannerheim than any Russian decoration he had received. Old General Carl Enckell, the superintendent of the School of Cadets at the time Mannerheim was expelled thirty-two years before, invited him to become an honorary member of the Old Cadets Club. Mannerheim was especially pleased because he liked the elderly officer.

Shortly after landing in Helsinki, Mannerheim saw danger for Finland: the "Red Guards," Finnish Communists supported by Russian soldiers, were about to take over the country. He believed that the Bolsheviks of Russia would enslave his countrymen.

Finland welcomed his help. Consequently, Mannerheim organized the White Guards in opposition, scraping together materials, weapons, and men, and he infused the White Guards with his formidable spirit.

A civil war boiled up, with Germany helping the Whites. Although the Red Guards and their Russian reinforcements outnumbered his army, Mannerheim led his raw soldiers to an amazing series of victories. But by the time the war ended, in May 1918, twenty-four thousand men had died, and the country had suffered widespread property damage.

Mannerheim is unique in history because of the varied positions he held. In 1919, he headed the new regime as Regent (Acting President), but he suffered defeat when he ran for President later in the year. In his retirement he worked to help the Finnish Red Cross and children who had been orphaned by the wars.

Turmoil was now Finland's enemy. The world war had hurt the country when the Allies blockaded its coast, and the barest existence became difficult. Mannerheim again performed for the country he loved by reconciling the Finns and the Allies and by securing loans for Allied support of Finland. This help became known quickly as "Mannerheim bread."

In 1939–1940 a "David-Goliath" war raged— Finland against Russia. It seemed as if the Finns had no chance against the colossus. But Mannerheim had previously erected the Mannerheim Line, a defense system on the Karelian Isthmus in southeastern Finland. For a while, the Finns astounded the world by beating the giant. They were able to do this because Mannerheim had insisted on discipline and careful training, because he knew the country better than the Russian generals did, and because he realized that the Finnish terrain, with its countless lakes and swamps, would baffle the Russian mass formations. He organized fast, small, hard-hitting units that cut into the Russians.

Sometimes Mannerheim's Finns slipped out of the forests on skis, dressed in white, the color of the snows that blanketed the landscape. The Russians were attacked by the white devils before they knew what had happened.

But eventually Russia won out by sheer size over Mannerheim's pigmy-sized forces.

When World War II blazed, the Finns fought Russia for revenge. In addition, they battled the Allies because the Germans tempted them with the thought that they could win back land they had lost to Russia in 1940.

In August 1944, with the war spelling disaster for Hitler, his countrymen, and his coalitions, Finland again turned to Mannerheim. The task was to extricate the country from the fighting. He accepted the presidency. With the rush of events, he was soon laboring to carry through difficult peace negotiations. Even with his adroit and smooth political work, Finland had to pay an indemnity of three hundred million dollars, and the Soviets took, under the treaty, territory, forest products, machinery, heavy equipment, and ships; but Finland remained a free nation.

Carl Mannerheim, the former cadet who was discharged for trying to fool the school authorities, closed his most unusual career by resigning the presidency in 1946. He died five years later. He is revered in his country as a soldier, patriot, and political leader without parallel, one who preserved his country's integrity.

MANFRED VON RICHTHOFEN
The Red Baron

SNOOPY, the remarkable dog who springs from the pen and wit of cartoonist Charles M. Schulz, is featured in the comic strip *Peanuts*. When Snoopy flies his Sopwith Camel in search of his arch enemy, the Red Baron, he sometimes slips into a malicious mood. As mysterious bullets zip out of the sky, Snoopy shouts angry curses at the Red Baron, who is somewhere aloft.

The Red Baron whom Snoopy shouts at was real. He was Manfred von Richthofen, the most dreaded ace of World War I.

No doubt if the Baron were alive he would enjoy Snoopy. Richthofen loved his Great Dane Moritz, who lived with him at airdromes back of the German lines. In his memoirs he called Moritz "the most beautiful being in all creation" and enjoyed telling him of his victories. Once Richthofen took him aloft, but the dog disliked flying. He did enjoy chasing planes as they taxied to the takeoff mark. This dangerous habit cost Moritz an ear when he ran close to a propeller. At least

Baron Manfred von Richthofen. (United Press International Photo)

Charles M. Schulz has spared Snoopy such an indignity.

Manfred von Richthofen, an alert blond of medium build, did not choose a military career, but was thrust into it. His father, a retired German army officer, made the decision and took his son, at the age of eleven, to the German military academy at Wahlstatt. Manfred disliked the rigid discipline; it felt like a halter around his neck. He yearned to be an individual, and that was the last thing the authorities at Wahlstatt wanted. But he found something there he did like: the thrill of danger when he and a friend risked their lives to climb the steeple on the town hall. They walked on the gutters near the tip in order to tie handkerchiefs to the pinnacle.

When Richthofen transferred to the less strict Lichterfelde Military Academy, he began to enjoy life because he was treated with more leniency. This was the same school that Erich Ludendorff had attended. Ludendorff's grades, however, were a plateau higher than those of Richthofen, who was a poor student.

The year 1911 found Richthofen a lieutenant in a cavalry regiment on the Russian border. He enjoyed riding, particularly the sense of mystic communication and feeling between a skilled horseman and his mount, but even more he loved freedom of action, something denied him at German military schools. As a cavalry platoon leader he was out on the ground almost daily, with fifteen uhlans jogging behind, doing his bidding instantly, and with no senior along to control him.

When war swept over Europe in 1914, Richthofen shared the Germans' enthusiasm for the hostilities. Here was danger coupled with opportunity to defend the fatherland. But he felt a tinge of jealousy. His brother Lothar, two years younger, also in the cavalry, was riding in front of one of the armies out to capture Paris. Manfred longed to be the hero of the family.

In early August 1914, Manfred had his own opportunity to fight on the then-exciting Western Front because he and his uhlans were transferred there. He anticipated action with pleasure, writing in his memoirs, "In my mind's eye, I saw myself at the head of a little troop sabering a hostile squadron, and was quite intoxicated with joyful expectation." He also wrote of a forty-mile horseback ride in a search for French soldiers. He felt proud to be in the foremost ranks that at any time might clash with the enemy. Although there was no fighting on the ride, anticipation of the peril was enough. Richthofen, who loved the superlative, called the ride "the most beautiful time of the war."

Mounted combat is indeed exciting. It turns on instant, almost instinctive decisions. There is no time to weigh alternatives, no time to ponder an estimate of the situation. But the war changed fighting methods. Richthofen's uhlans were ordered to dig trenches near Verdun. Pick-and-shovel work back of the lines seemed stupid to him, and it did not matter that the trenches might be used later. German authorities censored Richthofen's memoirs after the war, but they did not delete his distaste for boredom.

Richthofen soon remembered how thrilled he had been at the sight of an airman. Obviously, they did not dig trenches but had freedom of action in the skies. His thoughts led him to submit a request for a transfer to the Flying Service. It came back approved, and he jumped to the highest degree of excitement again, saying, "My greatest wish is fulfilled!"

Fred M. Reeder, once a skilled United States Navy pilot and flying instructor, has said, "Anyone can fly who is coordinated enough to dance, ride a bicycle, and play golf." Richthofen had no opportunity to play golf, but he was a marksman who could bring down swift-flying partridges and wild ducks. And, in addition to being a horseman, he was a gymnast.

But before Richthofen could become a pilot, he had to serve as an aerial observer on the Russian Front. There he experienced a narrow escape from death when he was in the rear seat behind Count von Holck, who piloted the plane through fire and smoke above a burning Russian town. The flight only whetted Richthofen's desire to pilot his own plane. Observers were definitely second team. When planes left the ground, it was the pilots who made the decisions.

On October 10, 1915, after a course at a flying school near Metz, Germany, Richthofen prepared to solo. The first flight alone is a never-to-be-forgotten event for any flier, and for Richthofen it was a turning point; he was determined to fight in the skies, not on the ground.

At the flight line that morning his flying instructor,

Lieutenant Zeumer, waited beside an old biplane. Zeumer waved carelessly at the plane and said, "It's yours, Richthofen. I think you can make it."

Richthofen's heart almost tore a hole in his leather jacket. He climbed into the cockpit, calmed himself, and checked the gas gauge. Before he knew it, he was aloft, the plane making its top speed of seventy miles an hour. The slipstream from the propeller lashed over the twelve-inch windshield and braced him. He felt contempt for death.

When Richthofen banked the plane toward the field in preparation for landing, the ship rushed toward a tree. He overcorrected. The plane crashed and nosed over. Zeumer ran up and pulled him from the wreckage. "I lost my balance," Richthofen explained.

The laughter and taunts of his fellow students stung Richthofen like bees. He tried again and failed. He began to dodge other students to escape embarrassment. He was a man who had to be superior in whatever he attempted. On Christmas Day, 1915, he finally passed and received the best Christmas present he ever had: his pilot's certificate.

Heaven was located on the Western Front for Richthofen. In March 1916, he began flying out of an airdrome near Verdun in a two-seater Albatros C III. The biplane had a Mercedes engine that could rev up 170 horsepower, to send the plane zipping through the skies at 87.5 miles an hour at about sea level, but its ceiling was limited to twelve thousand feet. Bolted to the cowling stood two machine guns.

Pilots of World War I specialized in "dogfights" — one pilot against the other — to the death. This caused the fliers to study and practice aerobatics, especially tight turns that let them swerve to the tail of an enemy plane, a desirable target because the ships carried no rear machine gun. Pilots who had the ability to make tight turns, and planes that could turn faster than others, possessed a tremendous advantage. The ships were highly maneuverable, more so than today's high-speed planes. Richthofen, searching for the best vehicle to use in dogfights, finally adopted the triplane because of the evolutions he could put it through.

The planes Richthofen and other pilots used possessed few instruments. The pilots received little protection from the elements and suffered in cold weather. Only a dozen years had passed since Wilbur and Orville Wright had made man's first flight in a heavier-than-air machine. Engineers were studying aerodynamics, endeavoring to develop planes that would fly higher and faster, while military leaders were trying to fathom the plane's role in war, in spite of what Marshal Ferdinand Foch said before hostilities began: "The airplane is all right for sport, but for war it is useless."

The early aviators were called "knights of the air" because during most of the war they fought their opponents in individual combat. Occasionally, in the early days of the fighting, adversaries saluted each other as they passed by. Writers seized on this. But aerial combat was not a knightly joust. Pilots aloft had to kill their opponents or be killed, just as hostile infantrymen do when they clash at close range. There was never any doubt in Richthofen's mind that to survive in a dogfight he had to be a better pilot and machine-gunner than his opponent.

Ground soldiers, living in mud or dust twenty-four hours a day, resented the "country-club warriors," who flew away from the fighting at dusk to comfortable beds in an airdrome. The thoughts of the ground soldiers failed to bother the fliers, least of all adventurers like Richthofen. He wanted to be in a fighter squadron ("chaser squadrons," the Germans called them) because the pilots usually flew single-seaters. You climbed into your cockpit and zoomed up to meet your adversary.

In late April of 1916, Richthofen, on duty with the Second Battle Squadron, sped from the airdrome near Verdun in his two-seater Albatros — on patrol. Out of an indigo cloud below flew a French Nieuport (its top speed was 107 miles an hour, faster than the Albatros). Richthofen held the advantage because of his height. He dove at the Frenchman, and it did not take him long to discover that something was wrong with the Frenchman's machine gun. Richthofen closed the gap between the two planes to a few yards, then opened up.

The Nieuport reared like a bucking bronco, then plunged lazily to earth, turning over and over. Richthofen followed to the treetops to make sure that his enemy was not trying an evasive trick. When the

French plane crashed, Richthofen felt a thrill of pride. At last he had a kill. But it was not recorded because the French pilot crashed in his own territory. There were no witnesses, other than Richthofen's observer, to confirm the crash.

In the summer of 1916, Richthofen traveled by train with his group back to the Eastern Front to endure the torture of a Russian summer. He found it exciting bombing Russian soldiers, with little fear from Russian planes or antiaircraft guns, but the big event of the summer was the arrival of the German ace Captain Oswald Boelcke.

Boelcke, who looked like an American college half-back or a professional lightweight boxer with the boxer's trademark, a battered nose, was known as the world's greatest combat pilot.

Each individual at Richthofen's drome in central and western Russia knew about Boelcke: how he had boasted, "On the Arabian Peninsula, I shot down an Englishman every morning before breakfast"; how he would cruise over enemy infantrymen after the completion of a reconnaissance flight and for recreation would pelt them with hand grenades; how he flew captured enemy planes to study their flight characteristics; and so on. He wore Germany's highest and most unusual decoration, the *Ordre pour le Mérite*.

The great Boelcke was not visiting airdromes on the Russian front for pleasure but was searching for talent. Richthofen, with his lithe, quick physique and alert mind, impressed him.

"How would you like to go with me," Boelcke asked, "and fight along the Somme?"

"Sir," Richthofen sputtered, "I never imagined. I'd be delighted to be your pupil."

Boelcke, a real leader, inspired his novices, none of whom had an official victory to their credit. So warm and natural was his personality, his pilots loved to be around him whether it was in the skies or in a school-room on the ground. One of the assets that helped make him the top German ace was his vision. It was always the beloved Boelcke who was first to see the specks in the sky that a few minutes later became hostile planes.

The Somme in 1916 delighted aggressive pilots like Boelcke and his pupil Richthofen. The British, who were trying to wrest air superiority from the Germans, kept from forty to sixty planes over the river from dawn until night. Dogfights developed every time Boelcke led his pilots off the runways.

The flights built in Richthofen respect for the British love for combat and for their brains, but most of all he hero-worshiped Boelcke. It was a star day in Richthofen's life when he returned from a dawn patrol to find Captain Boelcke seated at a breakfast table with some of the pilots. "Sir," Richthofen said to his teacher, "I report that I shot down an Englishman before breakfast."

One of Boelcke's pilots along the Somme in 1916 was the eighteen-year-old Max Immelmann, who relied on flying skill to bring down his opponents rather than the aggressiveness that became a Richthofen trademark. Immelmann was the celebrated inventor of the Immelmann Turn. To execute it, the aviator pulls back on the stick, sending the plane up on an arc, as if it were going to loop the loop. At the top of the circle, the pilot rolls his plane until he is upright and flies in the opposite direction from his original course. The Immelmann Turn was quickly copied by Allied fliers. It was fun to do, but the trouble was that in pulling up into the loop the plane lost speed and became a sitting duck for an enemy. The pilots in all air services, flying primitive planes, had to first nose the plane into a dangerous power dive to gain enough speed before it could execute an Immelmann.

At the end of October 1916, Richthofen lost his god. Boelcke went down in a freak accident when his plane touched the plane of a Royal Flying Corps pilot. Richthofen and his fellows were stunned. It seemed impossible that Boelcke could die. His pilots felt as if they had lost their best friend. They also felt intense anger at the British — anger that was not extinguished when Britons risked death to drop a wreath near his drome bearing a tag, "To the memory of Captain Boelcke, our brave and chivalrous foe," nor when they dropped a message extolling his bravery and apologizing for its late delivery because of bad weather.

On the death of the famous Boelcke, Richthofen became the scourge of the skies. In combat, he roared in regardless of the odds in order to fire the first shot, so important to a fighter pilot who is any kind of a

marksman. He downed Major L. G. Hawker, sometimes called the English Immelmann, who held the
Distinguished Service Order and the Victoria Cross.
Richthofen became a confident killer, and at the same
time tried to prepare himself for the day when his own
plane might go down. He wrote, "Nothing happens
without God's will. That is the only consolation which
any of us can put to our souls during this war."

When Richthofen had sixteen victims, he learned
that fame does not guarantee happiness. Fan mail
poured in, much of it from women. One even pro-
posed marriage. At first he answered the letters, then
their sheer number plus a new responsibility stopped
him. On November 25, 1916, he was appointed leader
of Boelcke's Chaser Squadron No. 16. Now he had to
think of others in addition to himself. But just as he
had enjoyed leading a file of fifteen cavalrymen, he was
happy telling other pilots what to do. In fact, he was
happier, he said, than he ever dreamed he could be. He
had not imagined that he would ever lead a
Richthofen squadron.

In the past when Richthofen let his thoughts concentrate on himself, as he did occasionally, he had
pouted. The high command of the German army was
either unfair or asleep; Boelcke and Immelmann had
won the *Ordre pour le Mérite* after shooting down
eight planes. He had sixteen victims and no coveted
medal.

Now, two days after assuming command of the
squadron, he was awarded the decoration by the

Kaiser. The skies above Richthofen's airdrome brightened. He wore the decoration close to his neck on all occasions and enjoyed the reaction of people when they first saw the rare medal.

In late 1916 Manfred von Richthofen was flying an Albatros D II; he liked it because it could stand punishment. He decided to paint this "packing case," as he called it, a brilliant red. His brother Lothar, who had quit the cavalry for the same reason he had and who was now in Squadron No. 16, painted his plane yellow. The other pilots seized on the idea. The varied colors of the squadron, and the fact that at times its planes moved on special trains from airdrome to airdrome, gave birth to the label "Richthofen's Flying Circus."

The German press began calling Richthofen the Red Battle Flier, and the Red Falcon. Only abroad was he called the Red Baron.

Richthofen was leading his pilots as cleverly and as fearlessly as Boelcke ever had. He set the example in the air. On the ground he was not as impressive. With a perverted sense of humor, he liked to walk through the barracks upsetting the beds of pilots who had earned a good night's rest.

Early in his career Richthofen had specialized in hunting down single enemy planes — a cripple limping home or a lone scout on reconnaissance. But in 1917 he began to apply a principle of war to great effect: appearing at the decisive point in greater numbers than the enemy. His success caused the British to organize the Anti-Richthofen Squadron. Richthofen took this not only as a compliment but as a huge joke. He confused the enemy by having a dozen planes in his circus painted red, like his own plane.

When Richthofen had fifty victories, he received a telegram saying that the Kaiser wanted to see him on May second. Manfred turned command of the Circus over to Lothar and flew to Cologne along the beautiful Rhine to the headquarters of the general staff at Kreuznach. The Kaiser looked him over as if he were an oddity and handed him a present — one the Kaiser liked — a large bust of himself. The Kaiser said, "Your birthday present, Richthofen. You are twenty-five today." The hero was suitably awed when he was introduced to General Ernst von Hoppener, leader of Flying Service, and to Germany's top generals, Hindenburg and Ludendorff. But in Schweidnitz, near Breslau, he received an equally great thrill: he was honored by his hometown Boy Scouts.

The ceremonies tendered by the Boy Scouts almost proved to be Richthofen's last honors. Back leading the Circus, he flew out of cumulus clouds in early July 1917 to see an enemy squadron a few miles away. He signaled his pilots to pretend to escape, in order to lure the foe into better positions. The British roared in. In the thirty-second eternity of the dogfight, Richthofen was shot in the head. His engine quit. He was momentarily stunned, and blood streamed over his face. He tore off his goggles. He realized that the plane was falling. By sheer will power he made himself look at the altimeter. He had descended nine thousand feet. In another thousand he would crash.

Richthofen righted the plane. It wobbled and glided across a field that had been so pockmarked by artillery shells that it resembled Swiss cheese. The plane barged through a maze of telephone wires, carried them along, and crashed. Richthofen fainted.

The best German doctors labored to save him. While he was recuperating, he wrote his book *The Red Battle Flier*. It was produced in huge quantities. Germans everywhere read it, even in the trenches. It is valuable because it describes his emotions and the rather simple life of World War I's top ace.

While gaining strength, Richthofen also devoted himself to his hobby of collecting souvenirs, which he shipped home to his mother for his den. The room looked like a disordered museum. Its walls and tables bore an iron stirrup, broken by a shrapnel ball, and a saber — relics of his cavalry days; a blown-up picture of himself in the cockpit of an Albatros Scout; photographs of other pilots; engraved silver cups bearing the names of his aerial kills; bits of fuselage; and numbered plates from planes he had shot down; and so on.

His mother and father were proud of their sons, the elderly major traveling to their airdrome with a telescope in the hope of seeing his boys shoot down an enemy plane.

Having fully recuperated, Richthofen downed his seventy-ninth and eightieth kills on Saturday, April 21, 1918. A band greeted him when his Fokker Dr. 1 triplane, the Red Devil, putt-putted in for a landing. He was not too pleased over such a show, and he was bored by the reporters who gathered about him for statements and by the press photographers who wanted him to pose looking at the sky. He was tired and looking forward to a leave, which he would spend hunting woodcock with a friend in the Black Forest.

On Sunday, Richthofen strode to the flight line. The Red Devil, all red except for a white tail, sounded good, its prop turning over easily. It carried sixteen gallons of gas, could make 122 miles an hour, and could zoom to twenty thousand feet. Richthofen wore a fur coat in cold weather, but now, with warmer air flowing into the hills near the Somme River, he wore coveralls over monogrammed pajamas and fur boots. It had been raining, but visibility was improving.

A mechanic stopped him and thrust forward a scrap of paper and a pencil. "Sir," he said, "your autograph, please. For my little boy."

Richthofen snapped, "What's the matter? Don't you think I'll come back?" Obviously he needed to hunt woodcock rather than Englishmen. He signed the paper, walked around his plane with a critical eye, shot a glance at five other pilots sitting in their planes, then pulled himself into the cockpit. In a few minutes he led the flight into the air. Mission: search for enemy planes and battle them along the river.

Aloft, the Red Baron did not have long to wait. Eight Sopwith Camels of the British Royal Flying Corps were boring through the clouds straight at his flight. He was joined by two friendly planes. A dogfight started, with the planes flying about like midges.

The wind screamed through the struts and wires of the Red Devil as Richthofen chased a Sopwith Camel piloted by Second Lieutenant Wilfred R. May. Richthofen dove after May, the two ships leveling off at two hundred feet. From the ground, Australian antiaircraft gunners poured machine-gun bullets into Richthofen's plane. So did Captain Arthur R. Brown, a jaunty Canadian, who darted in on Richthofen's tail to help May.

The Red Baron, caught in a crossfire of bullets, could not control the Red Devil. It staggered, glided a couple of hundred yards, nosed over, and crashed near the Australian gunners. So violent was the plane's impact that its propeller was never found. Richthofen was dead.

An autopsy showed that he had died as a result of a single bullet that had plowed through his chest. Almost immediately a dispute began. Who had shot Richthofen? Captain Brown reported that he had downed a "pure red triplane," and so did the Australians. The controversy has never been settled.

The Australian antiaircraft gunners buried Richthofen with the honors of war. Seven officers marched behind the casket, which was borne on a truck, a squad of buglers strutting in front. At Bertangles Cemetery, a chaplain and an Australian firing squad met the cortège and the flower-covered coffin.

Richthofen's death was top news all over the world. He was praised by Germans and by their foes. Allied airmen toasted him at banquets, but they were really happy that he was gone. The people who felt his death most, other than the members of the Richthofen family, were the men of his squadron.

In 1925 Richthofen's coffin was disinterred, taken to Germany, and carried through the streets of Berlin in great pomp and ceremony. It was reinterred in Invaliden Cemetery. Today, West Berliners cannot visit his grave because it lies in the Communist-held ground of East Berlin.

Manfred von Richthofen soon became a legend. His exploits were seized upon later and developed to inspire the Nazi air force. Playing a major part in this was Oberleutnant Hermann Göring, himself an ace. By the end of World War I Göring had downed twenty-two planes; he led the Richthofen Wing after Richthofen's death. However, when World War II began, chivalry in the skies quickly disappeared. Göring himself became one of Hitler's most despicable henchmen.

11

LAURENCE STALLINGS
Marine Who Never Quit Fighting

AT DAYBREAK, Lieutenant Larry Stallings peered over the sandbags along the top of his trench for his first glimpse of No-Man's-Land. The wrecked earth looked and smelled like a huge garbage dump. There was no sign of the enemy. A rat as big as a kitten skidded along the sandbags, then jumped down to the duckboards of the muddy trench and darted into a dugout.

"Jenkins," Stallings said to a private, in his soft Georgia drawl, "I wish you'd please go to regimental headquarters — turn left in the second trench — and borrow the ant bear."

The ant bear, who looked something like a huge raccoon but with a longer nose, was mascot for the Fifth Regiment of the United States Marines, who had brought him along from Haiti. Snapping and growling his way into the dugout, the ant bear destroyed rats.

"It's a genuine pleasure to watch him," the private said to Stallings. "From the looks of his work around here, this ant bear is the most valuable thing we got in the entire Marines."

The front-line trench cut through a quiet sector near Verdun in March 1918. When Stallings distributed his fifty-eight Marines along his trench, he told them, "They say we should get plenty of sleep in the daytime around here, and that it'll be boring. The nights are going to be hell."

Indeed, the nights were hell. Just after dark the German artillery cranked up, tossing shells toward the Allies' trenches, spraying the landscape with shrapnel and jagged fragments of iron. Allied artillery thundered back in counter-battery fire. A blockbuster exploding near Stallings coated him with mud. He felt frightened, but with his men looking at him he did his best to seem nonchalant.

On the third night, Larry Stallings received a hard mission. He read the curt order over and over:

TAKE THIRTY PICKED MEN. PROCEED ABOUT .7 MILE, DUE EAST. CUT WIRE IN FRONT OF GERMAN TRENCHES. DEPART: MIDNIGHT. RETURN: 4:30 A.M.

Cutting the barbed wire was routine in both armies, because with the wire down, an attack had a better chance of succeeding. Stallings believed that his Marines could carry out the job. He wondered, "How many men will this cost?"

Stallings inspected his patrol — the best men he had. He said, "Be alert. If we meet Germans, we'll avoid them. They're dangerous out there because their pa-

Laurence Stallings. (United Press International Photo)

trols are larger than ours. We believe that thirty is the best number for one of these night excursions."

At midnight, Larry Stallings and his men, their faces blackened, crawled over the top of the trench. Suddenly, the trench looked most inviting. Two American machine guns chattered nearby. A trench mortar coughed. Enemy star shells arched into the sky. When they burst, a tiny white parachute supported the burning flare to make it stay aloft longer. The flares, weird pendulums swinging back and forth, flooded No-Man's-Land with a ghastly, gray-green light. When the flares were up, Stallings' patrol remained motionless, flat on the ground, praying that they were unobserved.

After traveling across No-Man's-Land for what seemed an eternity, Stallings put his men in shell holes and hooded his flashlight. He looked at his watch. He had been out only twelve minutes. He whispered to his gunnery sergeant, "Hell, I forgot Rule One for night patrols: 'You've gone only half as far as you think you have.' "

When Stallings' men neared the enemy's barbed wire, they saw, in the light of a flare, the spiked helmet of a German sentry in a trench thirty yards away. It was like looking at death.

"Let me knock this heinie off with a grenade," the gunnery sergeant begged.

"No! We're here to cut wire," Stallings whispered.

The Marines worked in pairs, lying on their backs, one man gripping the barbed wire so that when it was cut it would not snap away with a bang, his partner wielding the wire cutter.

German flares shortened the wire-cutting time: the Marines couldn't work when No-Man's-Land looked like Broadway. Every few minutes an enemy machine gun sputtered its deadly *pop-pop-pop-pop*, sweeping the air just above the heads of the patrol with bullets. It was breathtaking duty.

When time came to go "home," Stallings solved the puzzle of finding passages in the American barbed-wire fences, and identified his patrol as friendly, so that it would not be fired on. When he and his exhausted men tumbled into their trench, he went in search of his captain.

"Sir," Stallings said, " 'porting back okay, sir. Mission accomplished. Didn't lose anybody. We worked for about two hours. I think each one of us should get the Croix de guerre, or at least a glass of beer."

After ten torturous days and nights in the trenches, the Second Division and its Marines withdrew to a rest area. It was a relief to be out of the stinking ditches. The men bathed, rested, received new uniforms, overhauled their equipment, and wrote letters home.

Back in 1916, Stallings had been a cub reporter on the Atlanta *Constitution*. He had enjoyed his work and performed it with ease. Then he received an assignment from his editor to "write about the U.S. Marines." A friend said at the time, "Larry was so inspired by his own writings, darned if he didn't up and join the Marines."

At Quantico, Virginia, Stallings found that training for a second lieutenant's commission was far tougher than the training he had undergone as an infantryman at Fort McClellan, Alabama, in the summers of his college years. There was then no war on the American horizon.

At Quantico, it was greet the dawn by standing reveille. Sweep barracks and clean up. Calisthenics before breakfast. Inspection. Attack. Defense. Withdrawal. Attack. Long days of physical exertion. Studying war.

Stallings enjoyed Sunday evenings at Quantico. He and other young Leathernecks gathered in the gym to sing songs led by a YMCA director. They sang the British war song "Tipperary," and the ridiculous "Good Morning, Mr. Zip-Zip-Zip!" a song about greeting bullets as they cracked merrily over the trenches. A favorite was "A Long, Long Trail." Another was a combat version of "Mary-Ann":

> *Keep your head down, Fritzy-boy,*
> *Keep your head down, Fritzy-boy,*
> *Late last night, in the pale moonlight*
> *We saw you, we saw you.*
> *You were fixing your old barbed wire*
> *When we opened rapid fire.*
> *If you want to see your father*
> *In the Fatherland*
> *Keep your head down, Fritzy-boy.*

After almost a year's training, Larry Stallings earned his gold bars. He became a Marine officer, intensely proud of the traditions of the Corps, his green uniform with its dignified bronze insignia, and the men he was assigned to lead.

Lieutenant Stallings was with the first Marine units rushed to France in the summer of 1917, and he was surprised to find life there dull. It proved to be a never-ending circle of guarding supply lines to the Front, training, and little time off. The highlight of his first few months was a review in honor of two of the war's top generals, Henri Pétain, the officer who had stopped the mutiny in the French army, and General John J. Pershing, the exacting leader of the American Expeditionary Force.

Stallings stood in the mass formation at the review, just behind the men in his platoon. Just ahead of him a private craned his neck to see a single-seater Sopwith Camel practicing aerobatics. Lieutenant Stallings cautioned softly, "Keep your eyes in ranks."

The regimental band lifted the men's hearts by playing the stirring "Marseillaise" and then "The Star-Spangled Banner." Out front, General Pétain saluted the Marines and said, "I congratulate you on your appearance and your behavior."

General Pershing, a staunch-looking soldier of great character, began to speak. Ever since arriving in France he had withstood pleas and pressure from French and British generals and politicians to feed American soldiers as replacements into decimated Allied units. And because Americans were in short supply of almost everything, General Pershing had had to beg from or barter with the French for artillery, heavy

ammunition, planes, horses, wagons, and other supplies for his army. In addition, he was plagued by a
fouled-up supply system in the United States.

To help straighten it out, Pershing had wired Washington:

RECOMMEND NO FURTHER SHIPMENTS OF FOLLOWING
ARTICLES: BATHTUBS, CABINETS, CHAIRS, EXCEPT FOLDING
CHAIRS, OFFICE DESKS, FLOOR WAX, STEP LADDERS, LAWN
MOWERS . . .

Pershing wrestled with even more burdensome problems, such as a scarcity of trained combat units. Now, at
the review, the AEF leader, who ordinarily showed no
more emotion than a steel cannon, shouted, "Congratulations! I only wish I had five hundred thousand
Marines."

Suddenly all the discomforts and tiresome duty
seemed worthwhile. Stallings could now smile at crossing the Atlantic on a ship that had zigzagged endlessly
to avoid German submarines, with Leathernecks
packed below decks like sardines, and the wearisome
train ride across France in dirty boxcars with high,
slatted sides, marked "40 men or 8 horses."

During their stay in a rest camp east of Paris, the
Marines — and the Allies — did not know that the war
was building to a crisis. General Ludendorff had secretly brought 262,000 German soldiers into the country on the Chemin des Dames, or "Ladies' Road," an
old carriage road that had been cut through a rough

forest area for the daughters of Louis XV. Ludendorff's hidden maneuver had deceived Marshal Ferdinand Foch, the Allies' generalissimo, and his staff.

On May 27, 1918, at Ludendorff's command, hell broke loose. German artillery smothered Allied artillery. The French army facing the Chemin des Dames was drenched with poison gas. The Germans smashed out of the woods and hurried toward Paris, city of their dreams, less than seventy miles away. They bent the Allied lines into a tremendous U by pushing with all their might on a thirty-mile front. Many French units dissolved, their soldiers running to the rear. Panic gripped Paris. About one million people deserted the city. It looked as if the Allies had lost the war.

The crisis distressed General Pershing. He rushed to Marshal Foch and offered him every available man. Consequently, the Second American Division, with its two regiments of Marines, hurried on foot and in supply trucks that had Chinese and French colonial drivers, to the Marne River.

The question was, "Could two American units, untested in fierce battle, stop the Germans?"

Lieutenant Laurence Stallings felt inadequate as the Marines swung down the road toward the front. He had been taught that Americans fight better when they know the situation. But what could he tell his platoon? Nothing except the obvious, as headlined in Paris newspaper: GERMANS POUND FOR PARIS.

The beautiful poplar-lined road from Paris to Château-Thierry cut through an unforgettable scene.

The road itself was reserved for men heading toward the Front. In the fields alongside streamed masses of civilians and French soldiers heading toward Paris with one thought in their minds: get away from the Germans. The civilians plodded along with dazed expressions, their belongings heaped in vehicles ranging from farm wagons to baby carriages. The old people and the children looked forlorn. Many of the French soldiers hurrying away from danger carried no weapons.

Someone yelled, "Gas!" and the Marines struggled into their masks.

The march went on. "I felt like I was eating grit with no air," Stallings said.

Hiking under full pack in the warm sunshine, wearing a mask, drenched him with sweat. Through the foggy goggles of the mask he could see a train of boxcars rumbling by on the railroad track paralleling the road; they were carrying wounded French soldiers to Paris.

Soon after the danger of a gas attack was over and the masks came off, French cavalry, smart in horizon-blue uniforms, clattered by, heading for Château-Thierry. It cheered Stallings to see Frenchmen riding toward the enemy.

A dull series of booms warned that combat was near. However, Stallings forgot the peril when from a hill-top he glimpsed the village of Château-Thierry, lovely even in ruins. Shortly, German shells began bursting around its Gothic tower, chipping away at its antiquity.

When the Marines plugged a gap in the faltering French lines near the village, Larry received his first bitter taste of battle. "But that was apple pie," he recalled, "compared to the month-long fight of our American infantrymen and artillery and Marines in and around close-by Belleau Wood."

The Germans had skillfully converted Belleau Wood, a natural fortress embracing five hills, into a strong point. They had cut lanes through the forest in a clever pattern so that hundreds of machine guns could send out streams of bullets unimpeded. Barbed-wire entanglements threaded the brush.

When Stallings read the order ". . . Belleau Wood must be captured," he felt as though he were reading a directive straight from Hell.

The assault began with American infantrymen fighting like demons on the flanks of the Marines. Near the end of June, the infantry colonel on the right flank sent the Marines a message, "I estimate that 4,000 gas shells have fallen on us. We have 855 casualties."

Confusion is a hallmark of every battle, and in Belleau Wood the Marines experienced it. Their mission of smashing straight into the German positions, as well as mistakes by a Marine lieutenant colonel in reading his map, added to the disorder and casualties. When hard-fighting German infantry succeeded in cutting off food and ammunition supplies to the Marines, the Leathernecks were in great danger. Trying to disengage from combat was like letting go of a bear.

In the late afternoon of June 25, 1918, Lieutenant Stallings and the Forty-seventh Company advanced up the slopes of the center hill to capture a strong point. The company's two hundred and fifty-six men had been whittled away by the Germans to seventy.

Stallings felt as if he were drowning. He staggered toward the enemy position followed by nine Marines. Belleau Wood, with its bent and broken tree trunks and dug-up earth, looked as if it had been hit by the wrath of God.

The explosion of a shell swayed Stallings and showered him with dirt and wood. Iron fragments bit into his leg. Another explosion rattled iron against his steel helmet and peppered his cheek. The sickly-sweet odor of mustard gas made him ill. His wrecked uniform was held together by string. Yet, around his waist and chest he, like other officers, wore a shiny leather Sam Browne belt, dubious bravado that advertised to the Germans, "I am a leader."

The nine Leathernecks pressed on Larry's heels as they toiled up the hill. Nearby, an enemy machine gun roared. Where was it? Suddenly, Stallings saw the gun defending its nest. He yanked his pistol from his shirt. A German officer rose out of the machine-gun entrenchment. He aimed his pistol at Stallings. Stallings fired at him, then fell. His right leg was on fire. He screamed.

When Stallings sat up and looked at his bloody, shattered leg, he saw medics tending the wounded with a captured German doctor helping. A navy first-aid man wound a tourniquet just above Larry's knee. Stallings was barely conscious as stretcher-bearers carried him from the wood on a litter made of two rifles and a blanket. A Model T ambulance stood by the side of the road, waiting.

Stallings felt relieved, as well as guilty, to be in the ambulance. Thankful to be heading out of the war, yet chagrined at leaving the fragment of his platoon. He tried to relax as the solid rubber tires jolted in and out of shell holes on the road back.

Blood from a young Marine on the stretcher over-head dripped on Larry's face. The boy said, "Lieu-tenant Stallings, I thank you for throwing me into that shell hole when we were at the gun. You saved my life. The doctor told me I'll be blind forever, but it's good to be alive."

The excitement had been so extreme that Stallings could not remember tossing anyone into a shell hole.

After eight torturous hours in the ambulance, with the tourniquet biting into his leg most of the time, surgeons examined Stallings. The tent hospital was quiet. A doctor handed Stallings a cup of coffee and said, "Mr. Stallings, I hate to tell you, but your leg has to come off below the knee. If we don't operate, gan-grene will get you. Amputation isn't the end of the road. They're doing wonderful things back in the States with artificial legs."

The operation sentenced Stallings to a bed and a wheelchair for a year. At first phantom pains racked him. He could feel his missing toes and ankle. But later severed nerves caused far worse neuroma pains.

In the long year, Stallings brooded. He hated war.

Not only had it crippled him, but it had taken wonderful comrades, and its blight had gripped his country. He despised writers who coated campaigns with glamour.

Near the end of the year in the hospital, Stallings learned to walk and climb stairs on his new wooden leg — "my Ohio willow," he jokingly called it. It took patience to have the socket fitted and refitted to his stump, scores and scores of times. Friction between the wooden leg and his stump caused painful sores. At first, he took pride in not limping, in not using a cane, and in seeing looks of amazement when people discovered that he was an amputee. He felt cheerful as long as he was with other amputees, but when he left the hospital to start civilian life again, his mood changed. His mind centered on the brutality and insensitiveness of war. He felt as if he had to expose its evils or burst.

Stallings sidetracked such thoughts for a time. At Georgetown University he studied the cultures of civilized peoples through their arts, religions, and languages, and earned a master's degree, but he did not bother to pick it up. What mattered more to him was exposing war.

Stallings did not rush into the mission he was setting for himself. He became an editor for the Washington *Times,* then moved to a copy desk on the New York *World,* where he advanced rapidly through the jobs of Sunday writer, editorial writer, and book reviewer.

When he was ready to go to work on war, he teamed up with the dramatist Maxwell Anderson. The two produced a stage play about Marines in World War I. Its locale was a French village in the path of war, and a front-line trench with its miserable dugout. The partners named their play *What Price Glory?*

What Price Glory? burst on the American theater in 1924 like a bomb. Audiences were totally unprepared for it. Many were offended by the coarse language and the gruesome scenes of the hard-bitten play. Senior Marines became upset. President Calvin Coolidge was furious and said that Stallings should be tried, but friends smoothed the matter over.

Not everyone recoiled. Young people left the theater feeling they had seen the truth about men in war. The dramatic critic Heywood Broun wrote, "This is certainly the best use the theater has yet made of war, and it is entirely possible that this is the best American play about anything."

Stallings next compiled and edited a collection of photographs of World War I entitled *The First World War: A Photographic History*. He exhibited a skill for pithy comments. For instance, underneath the picture of a civilian hanging by his neck from a pole, he wrote, "The Austrians Keep a Secret." No one can look at this book without feeling what Stallings intended: a revulsion against war.

By this time, Communists in the United States mistakenly believed that, with a little urging, Larry Stallings would join the Party. They worked to corral him, but he avoided them as if they were rattlesnakes.

He then wrote a newspaper column that carried him

to the attention of hundreds of thousands. He attacked everything he thought a violation of integrity or anything that did not measure up to his standards of Americanism. He joined the famous Algonquin Round Table group of artists and writers, but when two of the writers attacked him in print because they disliked his columns — strangely enough, they took aim at his leg instead of his prose — he felt outraged. But their sour remarks served an unusual end. Larry Stallings became an even wider-known celebrity.

In 1924 the Hollywood director King Vidor decided that, with Larry Stallings' help, he could produce a movie version of *What Price Glory?* Vidor signed Stallings to a contract and brought him from New York to Hollywood. While the train puffed its way across country, Stallings lay in the upper berth of a compartment telling Vidor about No-Man's-Land, Château-Thierry, and Belleau Wood. Stallings' artificial leg hung from a hook on the compartment wall, and when the train rumbled around a curve the artificial foot punctuated one of Stallings' remarks by clipping King Vidor on the chin. "It certainly emphasized one of the costs of war," Vidor said later.

Work by King Vidor, Irving Thalberg, Harry Behn, and Larry Stallings, as well as a host of actors and technicians, produced, in 1925, a film for Metro-Goldwyn-Mayer called *The Big Parade*. It made screen history.

The film was war set to "silent music." Some stroke of genius caused Vidor to secure a metronome. He trained the actor-soldiers to advance through Belleau

Wood, many of them in haunting silhouette, to the tempo of a funeral march. When music did accompany the action, its stirring chords meshed perfectly with the motions of the actors. Audiences sat entranced, moved and disturbed as they watched a ballet of death.

The film catapulted Stallings into greater fame, but life was not all roses. When he overdid, neuroma tortured his stump of a leg. Worse, he became the victim of an unhappy marriage. Bad fortune continued when a North Carolina plantation he had invested heavily in failed — and he had to undergo the agony of reamputation. Again he endured a long hospitalization. But Stallings bounced back.

In 1935 Larry and his wonderful second wife, Louise, were in North Africa at the time of the Italian invasion of Ethiopia. He became a war correspondent for the North American Newspaper Alliance syndicate and cabled his stories to America. They were penetrating and filled with understanding. His friend David C. ("Spec") McClure, a Hollywood author, wrote: "This odd figure, clumping over the wastelands of North Africa on his willow leg, had spent much of his postwar life studying military history and strategy. No longer a green, young lieutenant with a Sam Browne belt, he had a thorough understanding of the big picture of war, but it was humanized by an unfading memory of Belleau Wood, Château-Thierry, the moan of the wounded, and the utter finality of the dead."

Later, in Germany, Stallings saw the menacing iron heel of the Nazis. He recognized at once that another

war was in the making. He took the risk of facing a
Nazi firing squad by sending secret information about
Nazi military activities to the United States govern-
ment.

In 1940, when it was clear that the United States
would eventually enter World War II, Stallings again
volunteered. The Marine commandant asked him to
come to Washington, and once again Larry pulled on
the famous Marine uniform. How he passed a physical
examination, calling for two legs in good condition, is
still a mystery, but he did, and served in England in
the army air force as airman on the staff of General
Henry H. Arnold.

When World War II ended, Stallings' thoughts
returned to the battles he had experienced forty-five
years before. He wrote a comprehensive historical story
in easy-reading language, telling of how raw American
infantrymen — and Marines — fought in World War I.
This book, *The Doughboys*, begins with a blast at
President Woodrow Wilson who, when he attended
the Paris Peace Conference, failed to visit nearby
American battlefields. There are, however, light parts
in it about the grim business of war. For instance,
Stallings tells of a wounded infantryman, a Doughboy,
who, when offered a drink from an aid man's canteen,
said, "Give it to the Ourcq River. It needs it more
than I do."

Not long after the book's publication, Stallings
suffered the grievous misfortune of an arterial occlu-
sion in his "good" leg. He was rushed to the hospital

for the operation that dealt his nervous system a severe blow and that made him a double amputee.

When Stallings was able to receive visitors at home, Spec McClure came to cheer him up and to find out what he was up to. Afterwards, McClure wrote a farewell about the man who could not be slowed up by two wars or by two amputations: "[After my visit] I said good-by and walked with Louise down the stairs. But I had not got out of the door when I heard Stallings speaking at a fast clip. Knowing that he was alone, I looked curiously at Louise.

" 'He's talking to a tape recorder,' she explained with her fleeting smile. 'He's been working on a book about the Ethiopian War for years. From the sounds, he's in the home stretch. Laurence has a theory that dying is bad enough. But dying before you get your work done is positively indecent.' "

12

GEORGE C. MARSHALL
The Beginnings of a Great American

GEORGE MARSHALL was boiling mad. He had never been as angry in his seventeen years. He had just overheard his older brother Stuart say, "Mother, whatever you do, don't let George go to VMI. He'd disgrace the family." This was 1897.

George said to himself, "I'm going to smash Stuart in the face." Instead, he shoved his clenched hands into the pockets of his knickers and ran quietly upstairs to his room. He lit the lamp and glowered at himself in the mirror. He was as good as Stuart. Stuart was getting along all right as a chemist, but he had set no records at the Virginia Military Institute when he graduated three years back.

"Disgrace the family!" George was tired of hearing about the great Marshall family. His father preached about it all the time, usually starting off by bragging about Chief Justice John Marshall of the United States Supreme Court. Damn him! He had the advantage of being born in a log cabin. Then his father kept brag-

196

General George C. Marshall after he became a four-star general.
(United Press International Photo)

ging about Colonel Thomas Marshall, father of the Chief Justice, a surveyor in Indian country. There seemed to be no end to the Marshalls.

There was only one ancestor George relished: Blackbeard, a pirate with a horrible history. Once, when he told his father he liked Blackbeard, Mr. Marshall swelled up and snapped, "Ridiculous!" Later, when talking about his father's love for Marshall genealogy, George Marshall said, "All this talk was an irritation. The family history did not include *me*."

George and his father were not close. Mr. Marshall recognized this and tried to reach across the years to his son, but with intermittent success. George told himself, "Father's still back in Civil War times and doesn't understand modern goings-on." And George resented his father's almost complete absorption in the iron, coal, and coke business, and the time he spent away from home on affairs of the fraternal orders to which he belonged.

Mr. Marshall did take time out to go with George on occasional trout fishing and hunting trips in the beautiful Pennsylvania country around Uniontown. And once on a family picnic near old Fort Necessity, his father stood by the campfire and talked to Stuart, George, and their sister Marie about days in the French and Indian War, especially about Braddock's massacre. "After Father's talk," George said later, "I pictured Indians behind every tree. And we saw General Braddock's grave. I wanted to learn more history."

It was all very well for George to read history, but

his father kept pounding at him, with Stuart throwing in his two cents' worth, "If you don't bring up your arithmetic and spelling you'll be handicapped the rest of your life."

The pressure for George to do better in his studies started when he was five, when great Aunt Eliza Stuart came to live with the Marshalls. She didn't like the way George recited the ABC's — and his clumsy handwriting failed to round out. George got so that he hated to come home from school. He said later of Great Aunt Eliza, "She so soured me on studying and teaching that I liked never to have recovered from it."

There were other family problems affecting George. Mr. Marshall wanted him to grow into a lean spike of a man and hammered at him not to eat too much. He gave him an Episcopalian prayer book and a hymnal for doing without molasses. But the main trouble was school, from the elementary grades all the way through high school. When a report card came in, the house exploded. George couldn't talk to his mother about his low marks; she was as aloof as Queen Mary. Once his father became so furious over his mediocre work that he would not speak to him for several days. George felt as if sheets of ice covered the floors of their home instead of rugs. The more his father preached, the more miserable George grew. He shied away from people and became afraid of his father.

But it was fortunate that George overheard Stuart downgrading him, because it triggered desire to succeed. He said later, "The urge to succeed came from hearing Stuart's conversation with Mother. It had a psychological effect on my career." This urge, and the urge always to be first, never left George C. Marshall.

Although George detested the family history, it was the famous Marshall name that gained him entry into VMI. He was considering a military career. He knew he could get one through the Academy at West Point, New York, but that seemed as far off as the moon.

George knew about VMI and its superintendent, General Scott Shipp, nicknamed "Old Billy" by the cadets because of his white goatee. Shipp, a famous Confederate, had been wounded in the Civil War when he led the young VMI cadets against Union soldiers in the battle of New Market. And Old Billy knew the Marshalls. Why give George an examination when he was a relative of Colonel Charles Marshall, aide to General Robert E. Lee? So George Marshall sailed into VMI.

Marshall liked history, and VMI, in the legendary Shenandoah Valley, reeked with it. The spirit of General Stonewall Jackson hovered over the institute and the nearby Blue Ridge Mountains. He seemed a fitting god. As one of the best Confederate generals, this Old Testament–like soldier had not only been an instructor at VMI before the war, but during the fighting he led his "foot cavalry" up and down the valley, defeating four Union armies in thirty-nine days, each larger than his own.

George knew Jackson's campaigns by heart, and from Stuart Marshall he knew what to expect from life in the Spartan-like VMI barracks. Freshmen were called "Rats" and had no privileges. Room 88 met Stuart's "inventory": no rug, no pictures, a straight chair for each of the four occupants, four enameled basins (ice formed in them on cold mornings), a wardrobe to hang uniforms in, and four cots. Every morning after reveille the cadets rolled up their mattresses, strapped them, and stacked them ready for inspection in the corners of the room. The mattresses stayed there until bedtime.

It was not the Spartan customs that harassed Marshall, but upperclassmen. They were hornets. Marshall stood their hazing without trouble until one evening a sophomore barged into Room 88 and yelled, "Strip off your clothes, Rat Marshall!"

When George complied, the sophomore said, "Rat, sit on the point of this bayonet!" Marshall submitted, but after sitting a while in the strained position he felt ill and slipped, the bayonet knifing his buttocks.

The news flashed about the barracks. Upperclassmen worried. They feared a hazing investigation might expel them. Rat Marshall's wound obviously required treatment by the school doctor. What would the doctor report? But even though George had to miss drill, somehow he managed to keep it a secret from the doctor that he had been injured by a hazer. After this, to the delight of his three roommates, upperclassmen avoided Room 88.

The day the new cadets drew textbooks, George's worries began in earnest. His answer was to study every available minute, concentrating for the first time in his life. He had played baseball and football around Uniontown, and the VMI football coach and the team knew this, but Marshall said no to an invitation to try out for the squad. He was at VMI to do a job. He had no time now for either sport. He was anxious about his studies. George's classmates saw his problem, and some of them tutored him.

He began to pass examinations. Academic instructors realized that he could always be counted upon to try his best, and military instructors rated him as tops. When Rat year ended, George was chosen first corporal, to the surprise of no one. Now he began to learn about problems of leadership, the art of making people want to carry out orders. The next year he became first sergeant.

But Marshall made few friends, his shyness being mistaken for aloofness. It was hard to penetrate the armor of his reserve. However, his roommate Leonard K. Nicholson, took pains to dig beneath Marshall's tendency to draw back from others, and they became close. Later, Nicholson recalled:

"Puck Marshall — all Marshalls at VMI became Puck — I don't know why — we were friends and roommates for four years and never had a fight. When you got inside him, you learned he had a keen sense of humor, but he often hid it until we were alone.

"He was a natural leader. Once he said to me and Rooster [Robert W.] Johnson, 'Let's hike to the top of House Mountain and get back in time for dress parade. We'll use the regular infantry quick-step, marching uphill and down at one hundred and twenty paces to the minute, in cadence. No stopping or rests.'

" 'How far is it?' I asked.

"He said it was thirty miles, that he had scaled it off. It was closer to forty.

"Now Rooster and I did this because Puck wanted it. Time we got home, Rooster and I sought the doctor's care on account of blistered feet. But not Puck Marshall. He took his own blistered feet to parade and every formation, without a limp."

Puck Marshall loved the challenge, the fairness, and the orderliness of VMI life. He and his friends usually lived by the rules, but sometimes they took chances. Regulations required that cadets take turns weekly as room orderly — being responsible for the neatness and cleanliness of their rooms. As Nicholson related it years later: "Our scheme was for Puck and my other two roommates to do the work of room orderly while my name was posted showing I was it. I got the demerits awarded the room, but they furnished the sweat except when demerits piled up and I had to walk them off. Up and down carrying a gun, one hour for every five demerits, but it was worth it."

Nicholson went on: "I was proud of Puck. He held the highest cadet rank each year, and he *earned* the rank. In our last year he was First Captain, and he ran the job on the basis of fairness for all, a Marshall trademark.

"That year Puck felt confident enough in his studies

to go out for football, although he was six feet one and weighed only one forty-five. He played left guard for the Red, Yellow, and White as he did everything in life — hammer and tongs. In the game against Virginia Polytechnic Institute, he starred. Wish I could have seen it, but in those days when the team traveled the Corps stayed home."

The Rockbridge County *News* of Lexington, Virginia, described VMI's win in the traditional football game with VPI:

VMI 5 — VPI 0

The tackling of G. Marshall in breaking up interference was of the highest order, and a prominent University of Virginia athletic man said he was the best tackle in the south. The touchdown [5 points in 1900] was made by Johnson, left guard, believe it or not. . . .

The Cadet Corps, led by the band, marched to the station at 6 o'clock to welcome the team, and were joined by a great throng of people along the route, who surrounded the station and occupied the overlooking hill. When the train pulled in, the band playing "Dixie" almost drowned out the college yells of the cadets. Hundreds of sky rockets and Roman candles brightened the heavens. . . .

Suddenly, something happened to Marshall that had far more impact on him than football. He fell in love with Elizabeth ("Lilly") Carter Coles, who lived just outside the VMI Limit Gates. Vivacious and beautiful, she was four years older than George. When she appeared occasionally on the parade-ground road driving a pony and sitting up straight in a small carriage, his heart flipped over. Long ago, Lilly had been Stuart's date.

Graduation was less than six months away. First Captain Marshall was anxious to graduate, and going off limits might cause expulsion. This was 1901, and cadets received little time off. Even Saturday time off was limited. The only holidays were Christmas Day, New Year's Day, and Robert E. Lee's birthday. A very unsatisfactory situation. So First Captain Marshall took chances by "running the block" — going beyond limits without permission — to court Lilly. Fortunately he was not caught.

He and Lilly became engaged and were married the following February, after graduation. They left on a short honeymoon for Washington, D.C., he sporting a black Derby hat and a long brown overcoat, with a muffler around his neck; the bride wearing a fur-trimmed coat and carrying a fur muff.

In the meantime, Superintendent Shipp answered a query from Marshall's father: "Your son George is as well-qualified an officer of infantry as any man who has been turned out here. He will, in all respects, soon take his stand much above the average West Point graduate."

During Marshall's VMI years his interest in a military career had been clinched. One summer in Uniontown he saw the tumultuous welcome given returning veterans of the Spanish-American War, with the town's twenty thousand people lining the streets to honor and greet them. These soldiers, on parade, had fought for their country in the faraway Philippines. A military career not only seemed glamorous to George but useful to the United States. Years later he said, "I realized this small-town demonstration reflected pride . . . and the introduction of America into the affairs of the world beyond the seas." He was positive that he could lead men. With the help of the VMI authorities, he gained a second lieutenant's commission in the infantry.

The first order Marshall received brought sadness. He was to sail for the Philippines, but Lilly could not go with him because in those days no transportation was available for army wives.

In the Philippines Marshall not only missed Lilly, but he found tiresome the duty of clearing Mindoro Island of insurrectos, Filipinos who resisted the American occupation. To occupy himself between patrols, he studied the infantry profession with special attention to how battles were fought during the recent war. When orders came returning him to Fort Reno, near Oklahoma City, he was overjoyed because Lilly could join him.

But drab Fort Reno, surrounded by sagebrush and drenched in dust, a relic of Indian-fighting days, offered little except hunting. Consequently, Marshall applied his solution for dead-end military life: studying. And he and Lilly fought and barely won the battle of "living on a second lieutenant's pay divided by two." His salary was only $117 a month.

Suddenly Marshall was ordered to the army's command and general staff college at Fort Leavenworth, Kansas. This excited him; only the best officers were selected for the school. But he faced the same challenge he had conquered at VMI. Was he enough of a student? The answer involved his future in the army.

One day Marshall heard two fellow students making a list of officers who, in their opinion, would be selected to stay for the second year. "I was not on their list," Marshall said later, "and it made me furious. It was the old Stuart-like challenge all over again. I studied so hard that I couldn't sleep. I'd get up after I was in bed a few hours and shine and reshine my boots, something to occupy my mind."

By the end of the term at the staff college, not only was Marshall chosen to stay another year, but he ranked first in his class. At the conclusion of the second year the college kept him as an instructor for two more years. By the end of this time, 1910, thirteen years since he had entered VMI, Marshall had so developed his mind that he had absolute concentration and the ability to isolate a problem and to wrestle it to a conclusion — usually to a solution that proved correct.

But in one way Marshall paid for his development. He had few friends; only a handful called him George. Unless one knew him, like Cadet Nicholson, he was regarded as aloof, abrupt, and intense. He was far from a hail-fellow. Yet those who were his friends swore by him.

Senior officers recognized his ability. Lieutenant

Colonel Johnson Hagood wrote on Marshall's effi-
ciency report in 1916: "Captain Marshall should be
made a brigadier general, and every day this is post-
poned is a loss to the Army and the nation."

In 1916 the United States was drifting into the holo-
caust, and serious military officers like Marshall realized it. Allied propaganda, featuring stories of German
atrocities, flooded every state. Orders for war supplies
had been placed by Britain as early as 1915, and some
American manufacturers were on the road to becoming billionaires. German U-boats sent trade ships to
the bottom, carrying American sailors with them. The
sinking of the British liner *Lusitania*, in mid-1915, and
the death of one hundred and fourteen Americans, had
stunned people's minds. American public opinion was
blazing.

The Allied situation in 1916 was appalling. The
blood of Britain's best young men had seeped down a
swampy drain, and the shortage of food was grave.
British butcher shops, open only every other day, sold
out in an hour. The plight of France was even worse.
Children there had no milk. No one knew how many
millions of Russians had died, and the Czar's regime
was being toppled by the Communists.

The United States declared war against Germany on
April 6, 1917. President Wilson, in a burst of enthusiasm, called the country "the champion of mankind."
But the champion was not ready. It was almost power-
less to help the faltering Allies.

With war declared, Captain Marshall, now an aide

to Major General J. Franklin Bell on Governors Island
in New York Harbor, plunged into his new work of
organizing two training camps at Plattsburgh, in up-
state New York. The mission was to graduate twenty-
five hundred reserve officers every three months. These
men, called Ninety-Day Wonders by U.S. enlisted men,
proved invaluable to the United States. The work was
not easy. General Bell was ill. When Captain Marshall
cut fearlessly through red tape instead of carrying out
antique army regulations, he brought down the wrath
of senior staff officers. But he remained afloat by visiting General Bell daily in the hospital to tell him how
angry he was making older officers. General Bell
couldn't have cared less. He wanted the camps to func-
tion.

Like every officer worth his salt, Marshall was eager
to go overseas to fight. He had been trained for this,
and he believed that by fighting in France he could be
of greater help to the United States.

When General John J. Pershing came to Governors
Island in late May 1917, preparatory to sailing with
the first small contingent for France, Marshall reported to him.

Pershing was seated at a desk in Bell's headquarters,
a few papers spread before him. Across the front of his
desk lay his sword. The Spartan leader of the American
Expeditionary Force, fifty-eight years old, sat bolt upright. His crisp iron-gray mustache gave him a fierce
look, countered only by his small, twinkling blue eyes.

Marshall gave Pershing his best salute. "Sir," he said,

"Captain Marshall has permission to talk to General Pershing."

"Well?"

"Sir, I want to go overseas with you."

Pershing knew of Marshall and his top-drawer work, but he frowned. "You're on General Bell's staff."

"Yes, sir, but I've cleared this."

"I think General Bell needs you here."

Marshall was crestfallen, but a few months later Bell, who knew how much Marshall wanted to go to France, helped by securing for him a position on the staff of General William M. Sibert, leader of the First Division.

This unit was not a crack division at that time. Its ranks were a mixture of veterans of the fight against Villa along the Mexican border and the rawest recruits. Consequently, when the divison reported in France, General Pershing had to order more training for it.

When the harassed senior general of the AEF arrived a few months later to inspect the division's training camp one hundred and seventy miles southeast of Paris, he was not in a jovial mood. The First Division staged a mock attack on a "German" trench for Pershing. It was awful. Everything went wrong.

After the demonstration, General Pershing sent the soldiers back into camp and assembled the officers on a small hill where they could see the trench. "General Sibert," Pershing snapped, "step forward."

William Sibert, the division commander, stood in

front of his officers as unhappy as a man with a death in the family.

"Sibert," Pershing barked, "such an attack as you just staged would succeed only in getting a lot of men killed. Disgraceful! I saw no evidence of training. A blind man could see you haven't followed my directives. Where's your chief of staff?"

A colonel stepped out of the mass of officers, and Pershing roasted him. Then Pershing made a disgusted, downward sweep of his hands and stalked to his lead automobile. (He traveled with two cars, one available in case the other broke down.)

Captain Marshall was furious over what he considered unfair treatment. He thought General Pershing should know more facts, and he disliked his reprimanding General Sibert in front of the other officers. Marshall followed Pershing to his automobile and put his hand on the general's arm just as he yanked the door open.

"Just a minute, sir," Marshall said. "There's something you have to know, and I should say it. I've been here the longest."

Pershing set his jaw. "Well," he said, "what have *you* got to say?"

The crowd of officers stood aghast as Captain Marshall talked boldly to the god of the American Expeditionary Force, overwhelming him with a torrent of facts. He told Pershing why the maneuver against the trench was not up to par, and made him understand some of the problems of the division. "And," Marshall finished, "the chief of staff you reprimanded has been here only two days."

Pershing nodded to the driver, nodded at Marshall, and his cars putt-putted away. Then Sibert said sadly, "Marshall, I'm sorry you got in hot water for my sake."

Later a major said, "Marshall, Pershing has a mind like an elephant's. After the blast you gave him, it won't be long before you'll be headed for home on a slow boat."

"I don't know General Pershing," Marshall countered, "but I've heard he is always willing to listen to honest criticism."

Indeed, Pershing did not send Marshall back to the United States. After the division fought at close quarters in the village of Cantigny in May 1918, Pershing transferred Marshall, now a lieutenant colonel, to his own staff.

When the Allies straightened out a huge bulge in their lines in the early fall of 1918, capturing ground the Germans had held for four years at Saint-Mihiel, Marshall helped with the planning. He was not a headquarters-bound staff officer. He believed that he could do top planning work only if he knew the life the soldiers led. Consequently, he made trips to the front lines by car and on horseback to visit various trenches and dugouts. He came under artillery fire, but his principal duty of drawing up plans chained him, most of the time, to a desk.

His work was not easy. Every other piece of paper outlined a crisis. Suddenly, in mid-September of 1918,

General Hugh Drum, one of Pershing's chief assistants, handed Marshall a stupendous task: planning for the Meuse-Argonne offensive, the largest battle in American history up to that time. More than 1,200,000 soldiers would be involved. No such task had ever been dreamed of in the halls of the Fort Leavenworth staff college.

The gigantic planning problem sat squarely on Marshall's shoulders like a yoke of iron. He would have to give the necessary detailed orders in Pershing's name. Marshall checked all angles:

1. About 400,000 Americans will have to be moved secretly at night from the St.-Mihiel battlefield to the rough Meuse-Argonne country.

2. Some units are still fighting the enemy at St.-Mihiel.

3. Tired French and Italian divisions will have to be withdrawn from the Meuse-Argonne, and they must not block incoming units.

4. The road net is insufficient.

5. Trucks with drivers may be borrowed from the French. Some of the drivers will be Indo-Chinese. What about interpreters? What about gasoline and oil? There will not be enough trucks to move all of the 400,000. Some men will have to walk, but *by the start of the attack all units must be together.*

6. About 4,000 heavy cannon and 40,000 tons of ar-

tillery ammunition will have to be moved. More ammunition must follow without delay.

7. Horse-drawn and tractor-drawn artillery, as well as tanks, move at different speeds.

8. We have on hand about 93,000 horses and mules to pull supply wagons and equipment.

9. U.S. Engineers have necessary equipment and can lay railroad track and erect depots *provided* they are told immediately where these installations are to go.

10. Colonel William Mitchell must know the detailed plans in plenty of time so airplanes can help.

11. Thirty-four hospitals will have to be built, supplied, and doctors and Medical Corps men moved to them.

12. Wounded will have to be moved away from the battlefield, and in doing so there must be no interference with men and supplies moving up.

13. After attack starts, fifteen fresh divisions will have to be brought in from various parts of France. Arrangements?

14. All men and animals involved will require food.

15. Weather is turning cold and rainy. How will muddy roads affect the movement?

While George Marshall was studying the monstrous, seemingly insurmountable problem, General Drum walked in with the disheartening news that Marshal Foch thought the move to the Meuse-Argonne could not be accomplished in the ten days allotted. Drum added, "And Foch believes that the Germans will find out about it and will strike in the middle of the move."

For ten days and nights Marshall hardly slept. He ate at his desk and talked on the telephone until he was hoarse. But his orderly mind organized the enormous puzzle. Confusion existed on the roads, but the attack jumped off on time. American artillery churned up barbed wire and overpowered German fortifications. American infantrymen surged forward. Colonel Mitchell, the pioneer of American aviation, borrowed three hundred twenty-two planes from the French and grouped them into a single formation. They flew over the attacking American army and struck German reserves hidden in a wood, and downed German observation balloons. The coordinated Meuse-Argonne offensive was successful from the Allied point of view, and hastened the end of the war.

Later, in writing of his war experiences, Pershing penned a sentence about the Meuse-Argonne: "The details of the movements of troops connected with this concentration were worked out and their execution conducted under the able direction of Colonel George C. Marshall, Jr., of the Operations Section of the General Staff."

This terse declaration was balm for Marshall, and he felt almost as happy when Pershing selected him as his personal aide. After the war, the two made many trips around the United States.

The jaunts Marshall enjoyed most were a hunting

trip into the Adirondacks, and an excursion to New Orleans, where he saw his old VMI roommate. Leonard Nicholson, now president of the Times-Picayune Publishing Company, assembled his employees so a photographer could take a picture of the group with Pershing, Nicholson, and Marshall down front. Nicholson beamed as he told a reporter, "I knew all the time that Puck Marshall was a born soldier, a great soldier."

Yet Marshall felt disappointed with his progress in the army. The West Point song "Benny Havens" summed it up: "Promotion's very slow." Contemporaries like Douglas MacArthur were passing him in promotions. Consequently, Marshall seized a propitious moment to enlist Pershing's help. He wrote the general: "I'm fifty-four and still a colonel. If I don't get promoted soon, I'll never get anywhere in this army."

By this time Pershing believed in Marshall as firmly as Johnson Hagood did. The old general went to work, with the help of others, and in three years Lilly pinned a brigadier general's star on her husband's shoulder.

The record of the boy "who might disgrace the family" went on to be without parallel in the history of the country. He became chief of staff of the United States Army and a five-star general in World War II, after which knowledgeable people, headed by Winston Churchill, recognized him as "the architect of victory."

President Harry Truman appointed him his special representative with the rank of ambassador, and sent him to China. Later, as Secretary of State, Marshall put through the Marshall Plan. World War II had left Europe a bankrupt shambles. The plan brought food, housing, and tools to Europe so it could rebuild, and thwarted the Soviets in their aspirations to take over the European continent.

Marshall continued to serve his country as president of the Red Cross and Secretary of Defense, and was awarded the Nobel Peace Prize.

Probably the person who summed him up better than anyone was Paul Gray Hoffman, who helped administer the Marshall Plan. Hoffman knew Marshall's character when he said, "He was a tough-minded leader who never accepted good intentions as a substitute for results."

13

RALPH EATON
American First-Aid Man

IT LOOKED AS THOUGH Ralph Eaton, an eighteen-year-old United States Army recruit at Camp Logan, Texas, in 1917, might not eat Thanksgiving turkey and that he might be jugged in the post guardhouse. Everything depended upon the trial by the summary court-martial officer.

When Ralph had enlisted in Chicago, he had vowed silently to carry out orders, but how was he to know the army's customs? It had a million. Now he sat on a log, waiting for the officer's tent to open and reveal his fate, his moist hands smoothing out creases in his rough woolen olive-drab breeches.

A lieutenant in the tent barked, "Private Eaton."

Ralph walked in smartly, saluted as hard as he could, and fought to keep his knees still. The high, stand-up collar of his olive-drab blouse forced his chin to jut out awkwardly.

The lieutenant, a few years older than Ralph, rustled long sheets of paper on a table before him and

Ralph Eaton (right) with a friend, Philip Corcoran.

frowned. He straightened up on his camp stool and said, "Private Eaton, I'll read the charges against you, then I'll ask you how you plead. You are hereby warned that anything you say may be used against you. Do you understand?"

Ralph caught fragments of the charge. "Ninety-sixth Article of War . . . in that Private Ralph Parker Eaton, on duty as corporal of the guard, did show disrespect to the flag of the United States of America."

The lieutenant listened to Eaton's side of the story, scribbled a note, and said, "I find you guilty as charged. You are confined to the limits of the company street in this camp until the major sees you."

Later, an old major of the regular army, commanding the sanitary train at Camp Logan, sent for Ralph. In his hand the officer held the court-martial papers. "Eaton," he said in a tired voice, "I wish you'd tell me what the hell this is all about."

Eaton's words tumbled out, one on top of the other. "Sir, I was corporal of the guard. Two fellows helping me at retreat. We hauled the flag down slowly. I knew to do that. Then I said, 'Let's spread the flag out on the ground so we can do a good job folding it.' Lieutenant Werby dashed up and shouted, 'Don't let the flag touch the ground! You'll hear about this.' I didn't mean any disrespect, sir. I did not know it was wrong."

The major shook his head wearily and tore up the papers. "That's all, Eaton," he said.

Ralph sprinted for the mess hall. He could smell turkey and felt so good that he wished a track coach were timing him.

The army was hard for Eaton to understand. There were few explanations. It had been "Do this, do that!" ever since he enlisted to fight Germany.

Before that, he had been employed in Chicago by the Central Scientific Company, and existence had been precarious. The company had started him in its chemistry department at seven dollars a week. After three weeks, he received fifteen dollars, the boss saying, "We're raising you because you're a high school graduate. Keep your mouth shut about it."

Living in Chicago was a challenge. A weekly meal ticket — a card that was punched every time you ate a meal — cost five dollars, and you had to keep track of your credit. Ralph and his young friends in the company helped their budgets by strolling down State Street to the "down-and-out area," where a bowl of oatmeal cost ten cents, with a hunk of bread, a cup of coffee, and sugar free. When the room rent was paid, Ralph had little left. Fortunately, movies were only five cents, although it took ten cents to see *The Birth of a Nation.*

A few weeks in Chicago made Ralph wish he were back on his father's farm loading up on buckwheat flapjacks and floating them in homemade syrup or sorghum. "When my sister Pearl cooked 'em," he told a friend, "I ate a million. My mother died when I was two and Pearl, seventeen, took over my brother, my other sister — she was four — and me. Our farm in central Illinois was six miles out of Sidney, population four hundred. The farm and my father's work as a reporter kept us going. He was an Illinois University

graduate and had been editor of the *Pantagraph* newspaper, but that folded and money wasn't floating
around.

"Pearl had a world of pride. Unselfish. Worked most
of the time. Her pride was in the cleanliness of her
family. She devoted her life to us.

"When I was eight, Pearl handed me chores. It was
fill the cob bucket — we burned corncobs and sometimes coal, no wood any place around. Search for eggs
and bring them in intact. Clean the cows' stalls and try
to help in the stables with the horses and mules. But
Pearl saw to it that I had fun. She encouraged the
Eaton Brothers' battery, Howard catching, me twistin'
a curve. We played pick-up baseball, and I was happy
when we could scare up nine boys and some opposition. Father encouraged me in my collection of moths,
butterflies, and bird eggs.

"In the evenings, after I made a pass at my studies, it
was read and reread copies of the *Youth's Companion*,
St. Nicholas Magazine, and a magazine called *The
Hunter, Trader and Trapper*, until they were dog-
eared. We'd play cards, the whole family, but what we
really enjoyed was having Clarence Gardner drop in."

This was before TV and radio, and electricity had
not invaded the Eaton farm. Clarence Gardner, an old-
time teller of tall tales, often dropped in, and when he
did, Ralph sat fascinated on the edge of a straight-
backed cane-bottom kitchen chair.

Gardner would start off, "Last week, on a Saturday,
I was cooking ten pounds of rice for a pudding. The

rice began to swell, and before I knew it, it was all over the kitchen. It raised me two feet off the floor. I put it in pots, pans, and buckets and threw it out into the yard for the chickens and ducks. Wild snow geese spotted it and flew in. They darkened the sky. You should have heard 'em cackle when they spotted that rice. I got my gun. Started to shoot 'em, but they was so thick around me I couldn't. I used my gun as a club, and the ones I killed I sold for sixty dollars. I stuffed mattresses and pillows with their feathers. But things weren't okay. My cows started dying from eating too much wet clover. It's been a hectic day. I'm all worn out from digging graves for them." (And so on.)

Ralph said, "My brother Howard would howl with laughter, but I was younger and gullible and on fire to learn how things came out."

When Ralph grew older, he drove a horse and buggy to high school, his sister Berenice sitting by his side. He stabled the horse when they were in class. The twelve-mile round trip, four to six hours long depending on the weather, began in the dark in winter and ended in the dark. When icy winds moaned across the flat farmland, piling snowdrifts across the road, the trip became an ordeal.

Ralph's farm background seemed a light-year away as he walked through the Loop, the heart of Chicago's business district, in late April 1917. Fresh breezes from Lake Michigan seemed to carry excitement to every part of the city. A troop of mounted policemen rode by, the hooves of the horses clicking on the pavement. Behind them a band tooted "Over There." Long ranks of businessmen paraded by, filling the street, each man carrying a small American flag against his shoulder as if it were a gun. Applause and cheers from the crowds lining the curbs greeted the marchers.

At a corner farther into the Loop, an orator on a stepladder shouted, "Let's run every single German out of Chicago! We don't want spies. Look at what the Germans did to Belgium and Edith Cavell. What about the *Lusitania* murders? We will avenge them. Kaiser Wilhelm, when our boys go into action, your days are numbered!"

Flags crowded shop windows where placards advised young men to "Join the Colors" and advertised charitable affairs to raise money for war-ravaged peoples. A train of flatcars clattered on the elevated railroad, each bearing sailors and a float resembling a naval warship or a submarine. One car boasted a sign: U.S. NAVAL TRAINING STATION, GREAT LAKES.

Ralph recalled, "I didn't want the navy, but I was tired of being looked at because I wasn't in uniform. Firms were eager to have their young men enlist, so I quit the Scientific Company and walked into a Marine recruiting office. The Marine sergeant laughed at me. '*You* want to enlist? Why, buddy, you'd blow away in a good wind. Twenty-three skidoo.'

"I said, 'I've been ill for three months. I'll fatten up.'

" 'Okay,' he said, 'go fatten up and come back.' "

Ralph got a job at Chanute Airfield in central Illinois. It wasn't military service, but it was helping the country. Then he got wind that authorities at the University of Illinois were organizing a volunteer ambulance company, and because they had failed to fill their quota they were accepting young men who intended to enter the university.

"I held my hand up," he said, "and took the oath for the duration of the war. I soon found myself in a herd of boys on a train bound for Jefferson Barracks, Missouri. At railroad stations we were greeted by women who passed in cakes, sandwiches, and coffee. They treated us like heroes. But when we unloaded at Jefferson Barracks at twelve-thirty A.M., we were met by a runty corporal armed with a sawed-off pool cue. He gave us a rude greeting, barking at us like we were balky mules.

"This little grouch marched us to barracks and issued us each a cot and two blankets exactly the size of the cot. No mattress or pillow. We fell on the cots, exhausted, but at four, with no hint of the sun, he rousted us out and marched us to a railroad yard where we unloaded fifty-pound sacks of potatoes and placed them on mule-drawn escort wagons. At eight, he herded us to a huge mess hall, where we had breakfast. Cold, greasy, oven-fried potatoes — you could taste the pan — and gummy oatmeal with no milk, three thick slices of bread, no butter, and a cup of coffee black and strong enough to play 'Yankee Doodle.' I felt homesick. I kept thinking how I'd give all of the twenty-one dollars a month I would receive to sit once more in

Pearl's warm kitchen before a stack of her flapjacks.

"After breakfast, the corporal marched us to a clothing warehouse where they threw uniforms at us. When we left there, our arms full of clothing, he tried to make us keep step, and when a big mountaineer recruit from the Ozarks couldn't, the corporal stuck his sawed-off pool cue between the mountaineer's legs, and he fell flat on his face, his uniforms flapping into a mud puddle.

"The mountaineer jumped up and shouted, 'Don't you ever do that again. If you do, I'll jump down your throat and gallop your guts out.' The mountaineer was so fierce-looking and mad, and the corporal so runty and scared, this miniature czar avoided our group for the few days we stayed in Jefferson Barracks."

When the boys from Illinois learned that the idea of a University of Illinois ambulance company had been discarded, the bottom dropped out of everything. Ralph Eaton and four other boys were assigned to the Twenty-fifth Ambulance Company of the Fifth Infantry Division (regular army) and shipped on a train, two to a berth, to Fort Oglethorpe, Georgia.

The new routine was drill, drill, drill on a frosty, and occasionally snowy, parade ground. The "Sunny South" seemed a myth. To the recruits it appeared that the idea was to beat the Kaiser by performing perfect close-order drills. At times, they stood at rigid attention while instructors argued on how to proceed. Officers, almost as new as the recruits, checked continually on trivia: hat cords had to be sewn on campaign hats according to a diagram on the company bulletin board; blouse ornaments had to be arranged precisely, according to another drawing; wrap leggings had to be wound exactly right, and so on. When noncommissioned officers conducted the drills in order to give the officers a rest, it was obvious that not all of them had been selected because of their brains.

In the drafty tents, the talk was about the poor food, ill-fitting uniforms, and Europe-gone-mad. Eaton said that most of the recruits blamed the Kaiser for the war and guessed that when he was killed or captured it would end. Few knew its real causes. All believed that when General Pershing did get the army overseas he would show the Allies a trick or two about fighting. The sense of superiority over Europeans was very satisfying.

Orders sent Eaton and his four companions farther west to Camp Logan, Texas. It was here that he almost ran afoul of the Ninety-sixth Article of War when an unfeeling, inexperienced officer became upset over the way he folded the flag.

At Camp Logan the doctors of the ambulance company, most of whom had received their commissions as officers at the end of ninety days' military training, were handicapped because of lack of equipment. When they taught their men first aid, there were not enough bandages to go around. Stretchers were improvised so the aid men could be taught how to follow attacking infantry and how to carry wounded to the dressing station, as well as how to bring wounded into a trench from No-Man's-Land.

There were no ambulances. In order to teach how

they were to be loaded with wounded, outlines of ambulances were scratched in the dirt, and the dedicated doctors simulated the problem. At times the training was irksome, but the aid men developed pride in almost all their physicians, most of whom wore their uniforms more neatly than nearby infantry officers did. The aid men soon realized that they were better disciplined than the soldiers in some of the rifle companies of the division.

When the authorities decided that the Fifth Division had had enough training, it was ordered to France. The first step was a tiring train ride to Hoboken, New Jersey. The men felt uneasy as they climbed the gangplanks of the *Algonquin*, a British passenger liner converted to a troopship, but at the same time they felt glad to do their share for their country and hoped that they could help end the war.

Eaton wrote: "When the ship plowed New York Harbor at night, I just glimpsed the lights of the city because I was busy. I was working my way below decks, pushing through crowds of soldiers, exploring. For a country boy it was a thrill to be aboard an ocean liner. This feeling vanished as soon as we hit the first breakers. My stomach turned upside down.

"In the mess hall ninety tables, without legs or chairs, hung from the ceiling by chains. A ledge bordering the table kept dishes from sliding off. All meals were alike: two small rashers of bacon, two tablespoons of orange marmalade — you can sicken of that fast — a big, tasteless sea biscuit, and a cup of tea. The smell of steam and the roll of the ship made me stagger to my stateroom, where eight of us shared accommodations — double-decked bunks meant for four. At times I thought we were headed for the bottom and didn't care.

"By the time we staggered ashore, sped across England on a train that had no washrooms, and shipped on a dirty cattle boat across the English Channel to land at Le Havre, France, our own mothers wouldn't have claimed us."

At Le Havre, Ralph Eaton and his friend Tom Brady of Ventura, California, took advantage of a break and skidded for a café. They felt important when British Tommies saluted, thinking they were American officers. The two aid men were at a table, drinking champagne, when two American MPs entered and asked for their passes. When Eaton and Brady could not produce these, they were marched back to their company and turned over to the first sergeant, who assured the military policeman that they would be "taken care of."

"Nothing happened at first," Eaton said. "We rolled out of Le Havre in filthy boxcars marked *8 chevaux ou 40 hommes* (8 horses or 40 men) and finally unloaded at Saint-Dié in eastern France, near the Vosges Mountains. I assured Brady that the first sergeant had forgotten about us.

"But at the first assembly the first sergeant said, 'We're here for training, all but those wise guys, Eaton and Brady. They're for active duty in No-Man's-Land.

Eaton and Brady, get your packs and hoist yourselves into that truck. It'll carry you up to the Sixtieth Infantry. They're hanging onto a piece of trench.'

"My heart climbed into my mouth, and friends crowding around to wish us luck didn't help any." It was a high price to pay for half a glass of champagne.

When the two friends reported at the rear echelon of the Sixtieth Infantry, a runner escorted them to the front lines. They failed to notice that their guide was not wearing a steel helmet and was not carrying a gas mask. It was hot. Eaton and Brady perspired heavily from the weight of their packs, the thick woolen uniforms, and nervousness. They carried their gas masks in the alert position, just below their chins.

After a mile they arrived at a communication trench. The runner said, "Bend over low. The trench isn't deep enough, and there's a German sniper out there who can snuff out a candle at five hundred yards. We don't want any unpleasantness."

Eaton recounted later: "It's no joke to walk three hundred yards, under full pack, bent over like a crane searching for insects. The guide finally left us at a small ammunition dump. When Brady and I unloaded and crept around the trench to find out what was going on, the first American we came to had his woolen shirt off and was picking cooties [lice] off his undershirt. 'How far are we from the German lines?' I asked.

" 'They are at least two miles across the valley. This is a quiet sector save for a couple of blasts each night. In the daytime, the worst things are boredom and

working on this damned trench. I hear you two new-
comers are assigned in that first dugout near the communication trench.' "

Eaton and Brady staggered down the uneven steps of
the murky dugout. It was about seventeen feet square
and smelled dank. In several places water dripped from
the ceiling. It boasted a crude table, two ration boxes
that served as chairs, and a double-decked bunk of sag-
ging chicken wire made of two-by-fours. Brady unslung
his pack, and almost immediately a rat as big as a half-
grown rabbit started to gnaw on it. When Brady
cursed, drew his Medical Corps bolo, and charged it,
the rodent scrambled up a plank bracing the wall and
disappeared.

A first sergeant came in and shook hands. "I take it,"
he said, "that you two guys are replacements for Storke
and Halpin."

"No," Eaton said, "we're from the Twenty-fifth
Ambulance and are here on special duty."

Brady, who possessed as much curiosity as a fox terrier, asked, "What happened to those two fellows?"

"They just disappeared one night," the first sergeant
said. "It's my personal guess that a heinie patrol gobbled 'em up. They raid every so often for prisoners."

Brady went white. Eaton said later that his own face
did not look like a blushing rose.

Seven infantrymen lived with Eaton and Brady in
the dugout. The riflemen took turns carrying food
from rolling kitchens parked behind the trench sys-
tems, and made sure that the aid men had plenty to

eat. The infantrymen also assigned the aid men to the bunks. "We lived high," Eaton said, "because we were the guys who would care for them if they were wounded."

When it grew dark outside, Eaton climbed into the top bunk. It was hard to relax. His bones ached and, lying two feet below the ceiling, he felt as if he were in a huge grave. The riflemen spread blankets and curled up on the dirt floor, except for two who played cards by the light of a flickering candle. Shadows on the brown earth walls looked like the images of two giants. A rat ran along the edge of Eaton's bunk and a messkit, knife, fork, and spoon clattered down. The dugout became quiet, but in a little while Brady, who was in the lower bunk, screamed, "Damned rat ran across my face!"

The dugout door flapped open and a corporal called, "All right, Mulligan." The private scrambled into his equipment and up the rickety stairs to go on watch in the trench, a scene repeated every two hours.

Just before nine o'clock one of the card players announced, "Half minute to go. Hold on." Four terrific blasts in quick succession shook the dugout. Dirt rained on the men.

Brady spouted a string of oaths and said, "What in hell was that?"

"One-oh-fives," an infantryman said. "The heinies greet us with a salvo of high explosives from their howitzers each night promptly at nine and at one-thirty in the morning, to keep us interested in the war.

You can set your watch. That salvo probably hit about fifty yards away. It's like living in a roulette wheel waiting for your number to come up."

The third night, Eaton and Brady were ordered to accompany a patrol into No-Man's-Land. Their job was to carry a stretcher at the rear of the formation.

"After we passed through the American barbed wire and had traveled some distance," Eaton wrote, "the word whispered back that a German patrol had been spotted, that our leader would throw a hand grenade and would holler 'Run.' When the sergeant fired the grenade, Brady and I were the first to take off, but I guarantee you a half-dozen infantrymen tore by us as if we were shackled. I heard later that someone said a man cried out after the grenade was thrown, but I didn't hear anything because my ears were full of dirt kicked up by those passing us, and because I was concentrating on running bent over with my face practically on the ground."

When their nine-day front-line tour ended, Ralph Eaton and Tom Brady found themselves celebrities; no one else in the Twenty-fifth Ambulance had even smelled a front-line trench.

Four nights later, the first sergeant said, "Everyone get your equipment together because we're leaving this place and taking the road."

Someone called, "Where we going, Sarge?"

"To war," he answered.

This was typical. No one seemed to know anything; strategy was not explained to low-ranking officers,

NCOs, or privates; they just followed orders. Of the resulting action, Eaton wrote: "Corporal Dieffenback was killed, our first casualty. He was buried near Saint-Dié. His funeral was the first time I heard the bugle call taps. It tore my heart strings and still does. I never minded wounded people, but hate to be around dead people."

Eaton saw numbers of American and German dead during the Saint-Mihiel drive because the company helped support the attack. On one occasion, the aid men and doctors worked thirty-six hours with no rest. When rest did come, there was a poison-gas alert. Ralph Eaton pulled on his mask and fell asleep. "Mustard gas affects parts of the body which are damp," he said. "Wearing the mask caused me to perspire, and a whiff of gas seeped through, blistering my forehead. The hair never grew back, so my scalp receded, giving me an intellectual brow."

When the Meuse-Argonne offensive occurred, the Twenty-fifth Ambulance Company was among those moved in the massive and intricate shift from Saint-Mihiel to the Meuse-Argonne. Eaton described his experiences: "We were ordered to roll our packs and assemble near the highway to Verdun. A little after dark a French truck convoy appeared. The trucks were one-and-a-half tonners. Sides were slats and the tops were open. We were jammed like sardines, with four men in the aisle between seats. We moved en masse whenever the truck moved.

"The drivers were betelnut-chewing Indo-Chinese

and spoke no English. We took off, and I have never had such a ride in my life. It was pitch dark, and there were no lights on the trucks, yet the drivers drove like mad and frequently hit the truck ahead. The trucks were old, and creaked, cracked, groaned and wove from side to side, and we were certain they would disintegrate. When we hit a big chuckhole, which was often, one could almost see the slats on the side of the truck fly into space accompanied by soldiers.

"I was in the next-to-the-last truck, and when we had been traveling about an hour, it hit the truck ahead and the motor stalled. The truck behind us really smacked us. Our motor wouldn't start and both drivers, chattering like a couple of monkeys, worked on it and in a few minutes got it started. In the meantime the rest of the convoy had continued on its mad pace. We thought we had had a scary ride, but now we really took off bumpety-bump. At times it seemed we were on two wheels when we went around curves. How the trucks held together is a mystery. We finally caught up with the rest of the convoy, very much to our pleasure.

"A few minutes after passing through Verdun we stopped and assembled in a muddy field. It was raining hard, but in spite of it we could see and hear artillery fire not very much farther ahead.

"There was a battery of French artillery, long slender-barreled guns, probably about 4.5-inch, firing not more than a hundred yards from our assembly point. The place stank of mustard gas and the sweetish, sickening smell of decayed human flesh. I didn't know it, but we were camped on the Old Verdun battlefield where the Germans had lost a million men and the French almost as many."

Pressures of battle are fearful in headquarters, but they cannot equal the experiences of soldiers in the front line, where numbers are more important than names.

While the battle of the Meuse-Argonne blazed, another fight, of a different kind, went on just back of the front. Eaton and other aid men scouted No-Man's-Land, risking death to bring in the wounded. When a wounded man was discovered, he was given first aid and carried to the aid station on a stretcher.

Eaton recalled an episode of the battle: "After an attack, a bunch of us were resting, making hand-rolled Bull Durham cigarettes, when I noticed a pile of arms and legs outside the operating tent. Then a big truck rumbled up, heaped with dead. The men on it unloaded more arms and legs, as if they were so much cord wood, and when a head rolled out I lost interest fast."

Because Ralph Eaton was intelligent and conscientious, he was promoted to corporal. Then, in a few weeks, his surgeon, Lieutenant Kirk, sent for him. The doctor wore his uniform carelessly, blouse unbuttoned, a stethoscope dangling from his neck. "Eaton," he said, "I feel great that I can tell you you've been promoted to sergeant."

Eaton modestly told a friend, "I was promoted because Sergeant Adams was in poor health and had to be evacuated."

A rumor about an armistice excited the overworked doctors and aid men. When a staff car rolled up at night, its headlights blazing as if the car were on Broadway, Eaton believed it. But the rumors faded and the war seemed even more cruel. And in the distance the orchestra of the heavy guns, with red flashes against the night skies, served as reminders that more men were being killed and wounded.

Then a change came. Because help was needed at a field hospital, Lieutenant Kirk, Eaton, and several of his friends were transferred temporarily. In a huge tent, Sergeant Eaton and his team of one corporal and four privates laid out and sterilized instruments for the doctors, and when the surgeons rested, the team at times actually operated. "But," Eaton said, "the usual procedure was for Lieutenant Kirk to operate, stitch up the wound, then rest, while the corporal and I bandaged the poor soul."

When the work load lightened, at long last, Tom Brady sought out Ralph. "See here, *Sergeant* Eaton," he said, "I got a good idea. It's boring around here. How about you borrowing that half-ton truck and driving me and Hugh McCune and Egon Jones to the little café down at Verdun? The officers don't inspect after dark, and they'll never miss it. What they don't know won't hurt 'em, and besides we're entitled to some recreation."

The café wasn't lively, and Sergeant Eaton, who was not drinking, spent the evening trying to keep his friends from guzzling too much red wine. When he finally piled his crew into the truck and drove back to the motor pool, there, in the glare of the headlights, stood the officer of the day. In the morning, Ralph was a private.

There was talk among the officers that Ralph would soon be given back his sergeant's stripes, but the stripes were never restored.

When the Armistice was signed on November 11, 1918, the aid men breathed easily, but they soon developed an idea they talked about continually: "We enlisted for the duration; the war's over; when do we go home?"

Instead of being sent home the company traveled to Mondorf-les-Bains, north of the city of Luxembourg, as part of the United States Army of Occupation. Here the aid men lived in a theater and helped care for soldiers who had been stricken in an influenza epidemic. Ralph Eaton was assigned to the death chamber. There he had to comfort the dying and perform the work of an undertaker. After two nights he said to the lieutenant colonel, "Sir, you will have to court-martial me, but I'll be damned if I can stand any more of this work."

The senior officer assigned Ralph to a ward where prisoners were convalescing. This was almost as unpleasant. All of them faced long sentences. Ralph said, "I was unarmed, and frankly, I was afraid."

Two weeks later another company of aid men relieved Ralph's company, and now he and his friends enjoyed the hot sulfurous baths of the town. But existence in the unheated theater was miserable, and in the back of everyone's mind were thoughts of the dangerous flu epidemic. The thing that helped the men keep their equilibrium was baseball.

German boys, who had never seen the game, chased balls in the outfield at late-afternoon practice, but the boys tried to stop high-fly balls with their heads, as if they were playing soccer. "Our first practice was disastrous," Ralph said. "This was time off from the influenza patients, and here we were treating concussions and black eyes."

In September 1919, the long-looked-for orders arrived and the company sailed for home on the S.S. *Mauretania*. "Our spirits were up and it was de luxe," Eaton wrote. "Only four to a room. Up on A deck two hundred war brides promenaded, and after looking at them we thought the officers had poor taste. When we steamed into New York Harbor, we believed we were heroes and would receive a spectacular welcome, but the only greeting we got was when the crew of a tugboat threw oranges at us. For some reason, we thought this a poor token. We threw them back. We didn't realize New York had welcomed thousands of returning soldiers and the glamour had vanished.

"We were jammed into day coaches bound for Chicago and fed meals of corned beef, salmon, and hardtack. We thought at least we should have been rewarded with Pullmans and dining cars. Disillusionment set in like a plague. I finally was discharged almost a year after the signing of the Armistice. By this time my views of the United States Army were not very complimentary."

In early 1920, Eaton joined the ROTC with a view

of attending summer school at the University of Illinois. Captain William E. ("Wee") Burr, a perceptive officer on the lookout for outstanding enlisted men, singled out Ralph Eaton. "How would you like to go to West Point?" he asked.

"I don't want anything more about the army," Eaton answered.

"Get me your high school grades," Burr said.

Eaton did and forgot about the matter until one day he received a telegram from Washington ordering him to report to the United States Military Academy.

Ralph Eaton became a West Point cadet admired by contemporaries and officers alike because of his courage, modesty, wit, and desire to help people — traits he had evidenced as a first-aid man.

Eaton brought to West Point a salvaged first-aid kit "because," he said, "I didn't know what I was gettin' into. This small pack held scanty amounts of Brown's Cough Mixture, Argyrol (a local antiseptic), boric acid, iodine, ichthyol, zinc oxide, headache powder, CCC pills, castor oil, tape, and bandages, as well as a few throat swabs. I treated an ailing cadet. What did he do but recover, and spread the word that I was a medical genius. First thing I knew, I was running a dispensary in opposition to the West Point hospital and was called Doc. Fortunately, the authorities never found out."

"Doc" Eaton, poorly prepared and out of the habit of studying, worked tirelessly. He graduated in 1924 and was commissioned a second lieutenant in the infantry. He became well known in the army as an efficient, trustworthy officer.

On D-Day in World War II, Colonel Ralph Eaton sailed into Normandy, France, in a glider with other soldiers of the Eighty-second Airborne Division, during the first glider landing at night in history. In the crash, his hip was badly injured. But he recovered to serve as brigadier general and chief of staff to General Matthew B. Ridgway. Ridgway, one of the best leaders the American army has ever produced, wrote after the war: "Doc Eaton performed superior work. To me, he was the ideal chief of staff, and I shall ever be grateful for his incomparable service."

FOR FURTHER READING

I read many books and articles in the course of my research for this book. Space limitations prevent me from listing all of them. The ones that helped me the most follow.

GENERAL READING

DeWeerd, Harvey A. *Great Soldiers of the Two World Wars.* New York: Norton, 1941.

Esposito, Vincent J., chief ed. *The West Point Atlas of American Wars.* Vol. II: *1900–1953.* New York: Praeger, 1959.

Liddell-Hart, Basil Henry. *Reputations Ten Years After.* Boston: Little, Brown, 1928.

Reeder, Red. *The Story of the First World War.* New York: Hawthorn, 1962.

Reiners, Ludwig. *The Lamps Went Out in Europe.* New York: Pantheon, 1955.

Stamps, T. Dodson, and Vincent J. Esposito, eds. *A Short Military History of World War I* (with atlas). West Point, N.Y.: U.S. Military Academy, 1950.

THE DIFFERENCES BETWEEN WORLD WAR I AND WORLD WAR II

Mommsen, Wolfgang J. "Debate on German War Aims." In *1914: The Coming of the First World War.* Compiled by Walter L. Laqueur and George L. Morse. New York: Harper & Row, 1966.

Reeder, Red. *The Story of the Second World War: The Axis Strikes.*
New York: Hawthorn, 1969.
————. *The Story of the Second World War: The Allies Conquer.*
New York: Hawthorn, 1970.

ERICH LUDENDORFF

American Heritage, Editors of. *The American Heritage History of
World War I.* New York: Simon & Schuster, 1964.
Ludendorff, Erich von. *Ludendorff's Own Story.* New York: Harper,
1919.
Tshuppik, Karl. *Ludendorff.* Boston: Houghton Mifflin, 1932.

JOSEPH JOFFRE

Cameron, James. *1914.* New York: Rinehart, 1959.
Churchill, Allen. *Over Here!* New York: Dodd Mead, 1968.
*The Two Battles of the Marne: The Stories of Marshal Joffre, General
von Ludendorff, Marshal Foch, Crown Prince Wilhelm.* New York:
Cosmopolitan, 1927.

EDITH CAVELL

Cole, Margaret Isabel. *Women of Today.* Freeport, N.Y.: Books for
Libraries Press, 1968.
Graham, Evelyn. *Albert, King of the Belgians.* New York: Dodd, Mead,
1929.
Hoehling, A. A. *A Whisper of Eternity: The Mystery of Edith Cavell.*
New York: Thomas Yoseloff, 1957.
Judson, Helen. *Edith Cavell.* New York: Macmillan, 1941.
Mitchell, David J. *Monstrous Regiment: The Story of the First World
War.* New York: Macmillan, 1965.

FRITZ KREISLER

Elman, Mischa, Lino Francescatti, Yehudi Menuhin, Nathan Milstein,
Isaac Stern, and Joseph Szigeti. "The Kreisler Career." *Saturday
Review*, February 24, 1962.
Ewen, David. *American Composers Today.* New York: H. W. Wilson,
1949.
Kreisler, Fritz. *Four Weeks in the Trenches.* Boston: Houghton Mifflin,
1915.
Lochner, Louis Paul. *Fritz Kreisler.* New York: Macmillan, 1950.

WINSTON CHURCHILL

Bonham-Carter, Violet (Asquith). *Winston Churchill: An Intimate Portrait.* New York: Harcourt, Brace & World, 1965.

Churchill, Winston. *A Roving Commission: My Early Life.* New York: Scribner's, 1930.

Hough, Richard Alexander. *Admiral of the Fleet: The Life of John Fisher.* New York: Macmillan, 1970.

James, R. R. "The Politician." In *Churchill Revised.* New York: Dial, 1969.

New York *Times*, the staff of the. *Churchill.* New York: Bantam, 1965.

Taylor, A. J. P. "The Statesman." In *Churchill Revised.* New York: Dial, 1969.

Wibberley, Leonard. *The Life of Winston Churchill.* New York: Ariel, 1956.

Woods, Frederick, ed. *Young Winston's Wars: Original Despatches of Winston S. Churchill, War Correspondent, 1897–1900.* New York: Viking, 1973.

PHILIPPE PÉTAIN

Flanner, Janet. *Pétain, the Old Man of France.* New York: Simon & Schuster, 1944.

Griffiths, Richard. *Pétain.* Garden City, N.Y.: Doubleday, 1972.

Ryan, Stephen. *Pétain the Soldier.* South Brunswick, N.J.: A. S. Barnes, 1969.

Watt, Richard M. *Dare Call It Treason.* New York: Simon & Schuster, 1963.

WILLIAM BRECKENRIDGE

Nicholson, Gerald W. L. *Official History of the Canadian Army: Canadian Expeditionary Force, 1914–1919.* Ottawa: Department of National Defence, 1964.

Swettenham, John A. *To Seize the Victory.* Toronto: Ryerson, 1965.

CARL MANNERHEIM

Chamberlin, William Henry. *The Russian Revolution.* Vol. I: *1917–1918.* New York: Grosset & Dunlap, 1965.

Luckett, Richard. *The White Generals.* New York: Viking, 1971.

Mannerheim, Carl Gustaf. *The Memoirs of Marshal Mannerheim.* Translated by Count Eric Lewenhaupt. New York: Dutton, 1954.

MANFRED VON RICHTHOFEN

Burrows, William E. *Richthofen.* New York: Harcourt, Brace & World, 1969.

————. "To celebrate 50th Anniversary of Richthofen's death." *New York Times Magazine,* April 7, 1968.

Richthofen, Manfred F. von. *The Red Baron.* Edited by Stanley M. Ulanoff. Translated by Peter Kilduff. New York: Doubleday, 1969.

Titler, Dale M. *The Day the Red Baron Died.* New York: Walker, 1970.

LAURENCE STALLINGS

Asprey, Robert B. *At Belleau Wood.* New York: Putnam, 1965.

Metcalf, Clyde H. *A History of the United States Marine Corps.* New York: Putnam, 1939.

Stallings, Laurence. *The Doughboys: The Story of the A.E.F., 1917–1918.* New York: Harper & Row, 1963.

GEORGE C. MARSHALL

Carter, Marshall S. "Unforgettable George C. Marshall." *Reader's Digest,* July, 1972.

Pogue, Forrest C. *George C. Marshall: Education of a General.* New York: Viking, 1963.

Index